SNOWDEN'S STORY

To 2d Lieutenant
Ryan Martinez
Semper Fi!

SNOWDEN'S STORY

One Marine's Indebtedness
to the Corps

and very best wishes:

Lawrence F. Snowden

Lt. General Lawrence F. Snowden, USMC (Retired)

Lt Gen, USMC, Ret.

Turtle Cove Press
1837 Easton Forest Drive
Tallahassee, FL 32317
www.turtlecovepress.com

Except where otherwise credited, photographs appearing in this book are from the
personal collection of the author. Sincere appreciation to George Fong for allowing use
of his photo-graphs from events in Tallahassee, Florida, and to the American Chamber
of Commerce in Japan for permission to reproduce two journal covers that feature
General and Mrs. Snowden.

Printed in the United States of America

Library of Congress Control Number: In Progress

ISBN 978-0-9859438-4-4 (B&W)
ISBN 978-0-9859438-6-8 (Color)

Front cover photo: Lt. General Snowden, from his personal collection.

Back cover photo: General Snowden bows at the Iwo Jima Memorial, 14 March 2012.
Photo by Mass Communication Specialist 1st Class Johnnie Hickmon, U.S. Navy.

Back cover insets: Medals received on 18 March 2016: Department of the Navy
Distinguished Public Service Award (left) and Department of Defense Medal for
Distinguished Public Service (right), presented by General Robert B. Neller,
Commandant of the U.S. Marine Corps.

turtle cove press

Table of Contents

Preface...vii

Foreword viii

The Formative Years...1

Kindergarten and McGuffey School...14

Lane High School 18

Stetson University 26

The University of Virginia...29

World War II..34

    Marine Corps Base, Quantico, Virginia 35

    7th Candidates Class..36

    10th Reserve Officers Class 37

    Camp Lejeune, North Carolina...38

    Camp Pendleton, Oceanside, California................................40

    Roi and Namur Islands 40

    4th MarDiv Base Camp, Maui, Hawaii 41

    The West Loch Incident..41

    Saipan Island...42

    Tinian Island 43

    A Walk With Stephen Ambrose, Historian...........................44

    Workman Island (Code Name for Iwo Jima) 45

    Back to Base Camp on Maui..49

    Guam and the 3rd Marine Division..50

Between WWII and Korea 52

    Headquarters, U.S. Marine Corps,1946-1949.......................54

The Korean War...58

Marine Corps Recruiting Station, New York City 61

The United States European Command (EUCOM).....................66

The Senior School...72

HQMC 1959-1962 74

Commander, 3rd Battalion, 1st Marine Division and the Cuban

    Missile Crisis 79

Headquarters, Fleet Marine Force, Pacific: Pathway to Vietnam 86

My Vietnam Tour and the Industrial College of the Armed Forces...............94

The Big Selection Board and the Advanced Management Program,

    Graduate School of Business, Harvard University.................100

The Final Four 105

My Second Career: International Business 108
    Beirut 113
My Third and Final Career: Volunteering in Tallahassee.................118
Personal Anecdotes 123
    The Pool of Potential "Giants" 123
    My Memorable Moments with the Legendary Quartermaster General..124
    The Iwo Zero 126
    On Becoming a Marine Corps General Officer 127
    Our Small, Small World..134
My General Officer Assignments 138
    Brigadier General 138
    Director, Marine Corps Development Center................................139
    Major General, Chief of Staff, U.S. Forces, Japan........................142
    Marine Corps Operations Deputy to the Joint Chiefs of Staff..................145
    Chief of Staff, Headquarters, US Marine Corps...........................145
Reversion to the Snowden Clan 149
U.S.-Japan Attitude Change: Slow But Inevitable 155
The Reunion of Honor..161
The Declining Decade 165
Yes, There Can Be Hell on Earth..168
Appendices 173
    Appendix I..174
        Important Documents...174
    Appendix II 185
        Speech delivered 28 August 1962 185
    Appendix III...213
        Iwo Jima Battle Revisited, 2005 213
    Appendix IV 223
        Decorations and Medals* 223
About My Collaborator, M.R. Street..224

Preface

"You cannot exaggerate about the Marines. They are convinced to the point of arrogance that they are the most ferocious fighters on Earth, and the amusing thing about it is that that they are."

Father Kevin Kearney, 1st Marine Division Chaplain, Korean War

Lieutenant General Viktor Krulak, USMC, answering the question, "Why a Marine Corps?" concluded that America may not need a Marine Corps, but the nation wants a Marine Corps.

~~~

The chaplain was totally correct in his remarks, based on his exposure to Marines in war. General Krulak was a super Marine who never hesitated to tell it as he saw it.

In the pages that follow, I report on personal experiences which made my life in the Corps a most satisfying experience, and that experience was the root cause of my success in the international business career that followed, and even through my retirement years, where I continue to be active in several different fields.

The bottom line is that I am dedicated to the Marine Corps for what it did for me, and as I look back at my service, I wish I had done more for the Corps!

Foreword

Confession is said to be good for the soul, so it is a good idea for me to confess that I undertake the task of chronicling my life with a sense of futility on the one hand and a feeling of excitement and challenge on the other hand. Futility derives from my lack of confidence that I have the talent to write in a style that will attract even my closest family members to devote time to read about events in which they may or may not have been participants. Excitement and challenge derive from the fact that I really know that, compared to the careers and lives of a number of my friends, I have been fortunate to work with and become friends with heads of state, ambassadors, political leaders, and senior officers of the military services in the United States and other nations.

Martha and I wined and dined with world-known celebrities in some of the most prestigious resorts and restaurants in the world; and in our many years of working and living in the Far East, we lived a lifestyle worlds away from the modest small town environment that characterized our lives until after World War II.

Reaching the ninth decade of my life before starting this endeavor, it must be expected that my memory won't yield to my demands for details related to dates, names, and precise locations. My intentions are to report the incidents as best as I can remember, and I promise to resist the temptation to embellish my report in an effort to make a good story better.

Readers should expect that all the incidents which I report will be favorable to me. The fact is, I have had no unfavorable matters to report, and that amazes me as I look back over my life. Credit for that goes to my parents, who set high standards for me in my childhood days, and to the Marine Corps, which provided superb leaders for me when I moved into adulthood. Credit also goes to my dear wife, Martha, for her frugal ways when we lived through the lower grades of economic survival and her total acceptance of the idea that there were times when I placed the needs of the Marine Corps ahead of my family. We both agreed that my advancement in the Corps meant advancement for my family, and I truly was dedicated to both.

My two sons deserve credit also. Neither of them were ever in trouble in school or at home. They both grew up just ahead of the time when drug use among teenagers became a problem.

They both were athletically inclined, Steve in baseball and Brian in basketball. Even in those days, cigarettes and tobacco use were known to decrease lung capacity, and in their desires to be good athletes, they were not tempted. Even better, they decided that liquor did not taste good and they were not tempted.

Assuming I complete the outline I have in mind for this effort, I hope my grandchildren, great-grandchildren, and their offspring will recognize that if you will adopt a few simple rules (homilies) about basically trying to be a good person, follow some simple concepts about your work, live by them, and work hard to create your own good luck, you will enjoy more success than you thought possible when you are young!

The Formative Years

On the major roads leading into to the town of approximately 20,000 folks, several large billboards advertised "Charlottesville – In the heart of central Virginia." The town was best known as the home (Monticello) of Thomas Jefferson, the location of the University of Virginia (designed and original buildings supervised by Thomas Jefferson) and the home (Ash Lawn) of President James Monroe. I would like to claim that it was also known as my birthplace, but that requires me to stretch a little too far.

At approximately 2:30 a.m. on 14 April 1921, with the assistance of a midwife whose name I never knew, I arrived as the first (and only) born son of Lawrence Fontaine Snoddy and Beatrice Magnolia Snoddy, in a small apartment on the second floor over top of Graves Monument Company on Market Street, just a couple of buildings away from 4th Street, the site of the offices and printing plant of the Daily Progress, the town's one and only newspaper. At about age 12 or so I became a "paper boy" and delivered the newspaper to about forty customers along the Park Street/High Street area. I don't recall my weekly wages for that job but my mother thought I was underpaid and besides, it was late afternoon delivery and often made me late for supper and she did not like that either, so after a few months I was out of the newspaper business.

It was customary in those days for the first-born son to be named Junior after his Father and so it was in my case and on my birth certificate I was registered as Lawrence Fontaine Snoddy, Jr. It was not until I was a Brigadier General that I took the legal steps to return to the original family name of Snowden, and that will be covered later.

My Father, Lawrence, was born 25 October 1887 in the geographical area of Palmyra, a few miles outside of Scottsville, Virginia (about 26 miles southeast of Charlottesville). He was one of five sons born to Marion Ivan Snoddy and Martha Herndon Snoddy on a small farm. Following my father, there was Lewis, who had a long career as a Railway Conductor with the Baltimore and Ohio Railroad, based in Roanoke, Virginia. Then there was Elwyn, who died at an early age while the family was still on the farm. Then came John Lee, who worked for many years for the Chesapeake and Ohio Railroad and for years was their City Ticket Agent in Charlottesville. Marion Hermon was the youngest of the boys. He worked at a number of different jobs, married my mother Beatrice's (later called "BB") sister Nelda, and produced two of my double-first cousins, Marion Hermon Jr. and Robert O'Neill. (When brothers marry sisters, their offspring become double first cousins.)

On the road which ran alongside the farm, Grandfather Marion ran a small general store for a number of years. The store went out of business when the farm was sold, and he and Grandmother Mattie moved to Charlottesville. My father was the first to leave the farm for the big city, and he did it the hard way. At 18 years of age, he dropped out of school, walked to Charlottesville and went to work for Irving, Way, Hill Livery Stable. He tended the horses, cleaned harnesses and tack, and drove the livery wagons.

The wagons were sometimes pulled by one horse (two passengers on board) and sometimes pulled by two horses (four to six passengers). My father told me that he made countless number of trips in those livery wagons, hauling tourists up the unpaved road to Monticello, where he waited for them to view the house and grounds and then drove them back to downtown. Many tourists wanted to also visit Ash Lawn, and when that was the program, the trip took most of the day. About three quarters of the way up the mountain, there was an open spring alongside the road and it was a required stop. The spring water was always very cool and refreshing, and it provided a few minutes' rest for the passengers riding in the wagon over that unpaved road. That spring remained open and in its original state well into the 1940s, and Mimi, later wife Martha and I drank the pure, delicious water many times.

Over the years, as both the city and the livery stable grew, automobiles came along, the stable became an automobile agency, and my Father reportedly sold the first Chrysler in Charlottesville. When Mr. Way died, the business (Irving, Way, Hill) became Hill and Irving and remained under that title until one of Mr. Irving's sons became the manager and drove the business into bankruptcy. (He was a heavy drinker both off and on duty.)

With the help of a friend and a bank loan, my father bought the part of the business that became Irving and Snoddy Auto Body Shop, located on the corner of Third and Water Streets. Services included auto body repair, part or full body painting, custom making new tops for convertibles, installing seat covers or custom making them, and installing/replacing broken door glass and windshields.

It was truly a small business, with two primary employees, John and Carl Flick. John, the older of the two, was a remarkably talented man who was the savior of the business. John could estimate within a matter of a few inches how much material it would take to custom make a top for a convertible or how much paint it would take to put two coats of paint on a four-door sedan. When a customer wanted the pencil stripes along the doors and back through the trunk area, John did those by eye and by hand and there were never any wavy areas and they couldn't have been more perfect if applied by machine. He was a master of the heavy sewing machine which sewed the heavy canvas for the tops, and he sewed long seams straighter than robots do today. It is fair to say that, without John Flick, my Father's business venture would not have survived as long as it did.

Carl Flick was strictly a laborer who had to be instructed by John on what to do and then had to be checked on to insure that he did it. He much preferred to talk rather than sand a fender or grind down the edge of a door glass to make it fit. My Father treated the entire Flick family as if they were his family and did what was necessary to help them in times of sickness or financial difficulties. There were times when he could not pay them on Saturday afternoon because he did not have enough cash on hand but they were very understanding, having faith that he would pay them when he could. It was a very difficult situation for them when my Father's health required him to go out of business.

Most of Dad's customers paid cash, but there were some, mostly small businesses, who were billed monthly. After the second billing and there was no response, it was my job to deliver the bills and request that they provide at least a partial payment. I did not like that chore, but did it because I understood the need for it. Some of those customers did not like my personal delivery because, as one of them said to me, it put pressure on him at a time when it was not convenient to pay. My answer to that customer was that my Father's small business needed to save the postage (first-class postage stamps were three cents), and that as a small business he depended on prompt payment of bills due.

It was in the auto body shop that I learned my first lesson in business economics. A customer wanted a small replacement part for his car and it was not an item carried in the shop. Dad wanted to be helpful so he called the Blue Sonoco filling station across the street; they had the part so he told the customer he would send me over to get it. The customer handed my Dad three dollars so I could pay for the part which Dad was told would cost two dollars and thirty cents (that was the price to Dad, the wholesale price).

When I came back with the part, excited that I was doing business, I handed the part and the change (seventy cents) directly to the customer. After the customer left, Dad explained to me that he buys at wholesale and sells at a higher retail price. He explained that in this case, I should have handed the part and the change to him so he could add another twenty-five cents to the price paid by the customer. That twenty-five cents was money he was entitled to for finding and delivering the part to the customer. The lesson I learned was that despite my eagerness to participate in the transaction, I did not know the rules of the game and should not have interacted directly with the customer.

Even before that experience, I learned a valuable lesson from my Mother, an experience which I call my Red Apple incident. Walking home from school one day at age six, I took a short cut through Gleason's Grocery Store. While there, I saw one of our City Police Officers pick up a large red apple, bite into it and eating it as he walked out of the store without paying for it. So, I did the same thing and was just finishing it as I reached home.

Mother asked, "Where did you get that apple?"

I told her I did what the policeman did.

Knowing that I did not have any money, she asked, "Did you pay for it?"

I said, "No ma'am."

She went to her purse, pulled out a dime and said, "You must pay for that apple, so you go back to the store, find Mr. Gleason, tell him you are sorry for what you did and that it will never happen again. Do you understand?"

I said, "Yes, Ma'am," and started walking.

Mr. Gleason had his office on an upstairs floor which looked out over the main floor of the stored. He saw me and waved for me to come up there. I extended my hand to give him the dime. He said, "Your Mother called me and explained the situation. I can understand why you thought the apples were free. So, as a reward for your apology, you do not have to pay for the apple."

I said, "Mr. Gleason, my Mother said I have to pay for the apple," as I extended my hand again.

He said, "All right," took the dime, and handed me back a nickel. I headed home with a joyful step, with a lesson learned.

The Hill and Irving business which evolved into a Chrysler Dealership included a funeral parlor, a couple of blocks further west on Main Street. My Father used to help out at the funeral home, sometimes assisting in the embalming process, seating folks at the funeral service and then driving the hearse to the cemetery. With that experience, when he went into the Army in World War I, he was assigned to the Medical Corps and immediately sent to Fort Sherman, Ohio because the Army was suffering a major flu epidemic at that site. He spent all of his active duty time at that site but had attained the rank of Sergeant at the time of his discharge. He always lamented the fact that he did not serve overseas like his brother Hermon did.

The Peoples National Bank was right across the street from my father's auto body business. Most of the bank workers, from the President on down to the young girl tellers, used to call him "Sunshine." He was in that bank almost every day, sometimes just passing through as he was headed up to Timberlake's Drugstore for a mid-morning cup of coffee. On many of those mornings, some of the young girls in the bank would ask him to bring them a cup of coffee on his way back from the drugstore and he always fulfilled their requests.

As you might guess, my Mother was not thrilled with those young girls calling him Sunshine and she was not happy at the idea of him carrying six or seven cups of coffee to them. She thought they were taking advantage of his good nature, and indeed they were, but she recognized that he was somewhat flattered by the friendly relationships of all those Bank folks, so she expressed her displeasure to me but not to anyone else.

Unfortunately, my Father started smoking cigarettes at an early age. In those days, it was the manly thing to do, and certainly, no one thought smoking was unhealthy. In later years, he switched to cigars, usually the five-cent El Productos.

When, as a Marine, I began to move about in the world, I would sometimes bring him a box of high quality, more expensive cigars. Though I was generally a nonsmoker (I never was a cigarette smoker), I would sit with him and smoke one of the new cigars. We enjoyed the time together and he always said that the cigars were very good.

After his death, when Mother and I were clearing some closets where some of his things were stored, we found about ten boxes of the cigars I had brought to him. He had received them graciously and I think he enjoyed the cigar-sharing time with me, but it was clear that, when my visit was over, he put the fancy cigars away and went back to smoking his favorite five-cent El Productos!

As we know now, smoking can bring on emphysema, damage the lungs, and cause severe breathing problems. It was distressing to watch this tall, handsome man become so thin and feeble. He was admitted to the Veterans Administration Hospital in Richmond, Virginia, and after a number of months there, the lung problem caused his death. I was serving in Hawaii at the time at Headquarters, Fleet Marine Forces, Pacific but was able to leave for home within hours of notification of his death.

His hospitalization in Richmond was a real hardship on my Mother who was dedicated to visiting him at least one day each week. It required a full day to go by bus, get a taxi from the bus station to the hospital, visit with him for a few hours, then reverse the procedure to get back home. She never complained about the trip, but it was very physically tiring and, because of his deteriorating condition, it was an emotional strain.

Before leaving for Hawaii, I had visited with him in the hospital and left him knowing that it would be our last time together. We accepted his death as a way to stop his pain and gain peace for his soul. He never gained the economic success he had hoped for, but he was a handsome, well-dressed gentleman who was loved by many folks in his community. Those bank folks from across the street wrote my father a lot of notes while he was in the hospital.

Beatrice Magnolia Huffman was born on 12 May 1887, the first-born child of Stuart Ryder Huffman and Nora O'Neill Huffman, in Greenville, Virginia, a small town close to the Virginia-West Virginia border. On the marriage license, her birthplace is shown as Charlottesville, but she insisted she was born in Greenville. Mother used to tell me that many folks in that area did not know which state they

lived in, but when they had to put it in writing, almost all of them chose
Virginia.

Grandfather Huffman was a ruggedly handsome man who
claimed to be a stonemason, a title that he considered superior to brick
layer. He was a specialist in creating archways, fancy brick or stone
columns at entrances to big farms and estates. At one point, he helped
restore a section of the serpentine wall at the University of Virginia, a job
which gave him wide recognition as a Master Brick Layer because the
section of wall which he restored matched the original wall so well that
most folks could not tell the restored from the original.

Grandmother Nora gave birth to two sons and three daughters in
addition to my mother. Mother (Beatrice, later called BB by everyone in
the family) was the oldest, followed by Carlyle, Stuart, Mable, Nelda, and
Thelma. Carlyle had the good looks of his father and had a long career
with the Washington, D.C. Police Department, serving as a Detective at
the time of his death. Stuart was a tile setter and did the installation of
decorative tiles on ships under construction at the Norfolk shipyards.
Mable married James Banks, a machinist with a couple of railroads in
Richmond, Virginia. He was Uncle Jimmy to me and was a superb artist.
At one time, he painted oil portraits of each Virginia State Trooper killed
in the line of duty. Those portraits were hung in the State Capitol
Building.

Nelda married my father's brother Hermon, and they lived with
us from time to time. After Uncle Hermon's death, Nelda lived with BB
for several years before Hermon Jr. and his brother Robert (always Bobby
to me) relocated her to a small apartment near where Hermon Jr. lived,
just off Locust Avenue. In recent years, he preferred to be called Marion.
Marion was a retired Certified Public Accountant and Robert is a retired
Pharmacist.

Thelma married Roy Davis, and they had one child, Bette Lee
Davis. I suggested that name and they accepted it. That marriage did not
last very long, and they divorced. It was necessary for Thelma to work,
so Bette essentially was raised by her Grandmother Nora. Unfortunately,

Nora was ultra-protective of Bette, never let her loose from her apron strings, and it was a most unhappy relationship for Bette. Years later, Thelma married Ernest Minson, a financial officer for a major lumber company in Richmond, Virginia. After his retirement, they relocated to Los Angeles where they remained until their deaths. Ernest died first and Thelma lived alone in their apartment in Westwood. Bette lived in an apartment in the same complex, and she looked after Thelma until her death. Bette continues to live in the Los Angeles area where she is in the industrial facility design and decorating business.

BB was always the matriarch of the family, even when Nora was living. Nora married Henry Pitzer, who operated a billiard parlor in Lexington, Virginia, patronized by students of Washington and Lee University and the Virginia Military Institute. While he made a respectful living with the billiard parlor, he and Nora made no financial contributions to the rest of the family. Family members who had problems always came to talk to BB and various members of the family lived with us from time to time when they were in between jobs or places to live.

John and Bessie lived with us when they were first married, and so did Hermon and Nelda. Thelma lived with us when she was working in Charlottesville and was being courted by Roy Davis. As noted earlier, Nelda lived with my parents for quite a while after Uncle Hermon died.

Even while he was still working for Hill and Irving, my father had a working relationship with Mr. Horace Twyman. Horace and Fred Twyman were brothers, both quite successful financially in Charlottesville. Fred was a lawyer and Horace was a bachelor who managed the two theaters they owned, the Jefferson Theater and the Lafayette Theater, both on Main Street in downtown Charlottesville. They later added the University Theater near the grounds of the University of Virginia. My Father was kind of an on-call handyman at those theaters, sometimes being the ticket taker, sometimes being the ticket seller, or doing whatever needed to be done at the moment.

Horace was not very tall, rotund, red faced and a tough

businessman. He always owned Buick automobiles but would only drive locally. When he went on a trip, he wanted my father to drive for him; that is how the relationship started. Horace liked his nip of bourbon (sometimes local "moonshine"), and my Father was not a drinker, so it was a good pairing. One of my early memories was when Dad drove Horace to Canada for the World's Fair. Over time, Horace became a close friend of the family.

As a bachelor, Horace lived in several different boarding houses, and in 1935, he made the following offer to my parents. He would build a house on Evergreen Avenue which would include an apartment for him, and the rest of the house was for us. Originally, he said he would take his meals elsewhere, but that soon changed to him being a full-time boarder. His original proposal was that after he died, it would continue to be our house until the death of my mother. Further, he would set up a trust fund to pay the maintenance expenses on the house. Sounds like a great deal, doesn't it? It was for a while, but then the burden began to fall on my mother. She felt she was obligated to prepare three meals a day, and that limited the amount of time available to go to the movies, shopping, or whatever else she might want to do.

Horace had a number of old cronies he liked to invite over for poker, and they played down in the basement of the Evergreen Avenue house. The basement had a finished concrete floor, a toilet and washbasin, a laundry room, and a furnace room which led out to the single-car garage. BB always felt she must have the whole basement clean and in good order when the card games were on, frequently on short notice. She always had to prepare a tray of snacks to go along with whatever beverages they had.

Horace had a pretty good set-up. His apartment, upstairs on the right-hand side of the house, had a sitting room, a very large bedroom, and an unusually large bathroom. He had maid service provided by BB, and had his laundry done by a colored lady who stopped by each week to pick up and deliver his laundered shirts and other items. When there was a need, my father was available as his driver. He had heart problems, and a couple of years before his death, he had a master bedroom constructed on the back of the house. There, in the middle of the night, he passed away.

In later years, after living in a dormitory as required of first-year men at the University, Brian occupied that spacious apartment while he was a student at the University of Virginia. He enjoyed the same maid service from BB that she had provided to Horace Twyman and, additionally, she provided laundry service to him.

Horace Twyman's intentions were good about setting up a trust fund to take care of the maintenance of the house, but he failed to take into account that maintenance costs would rise as the house grew older. Through his Will, he established a trust fund in the Peoples Bank with instructions that the income to the trust would be used to defray the maintenance costs on the house. The principal sum of the trust was too small, and within a few years, the burden of the repairs and maintenance costs fell on my family, and my family was not economically prepared to accept those expenses.

My mother's solution was to take out a small loan from the bank and pay each month as she could afford. Sometimes she could only pay the interest due and paid nothing to reduce the principal of the loan. Mr. Mason Byrd, a neighbor on Evergreen Avenue and an old friend of the family, was the administrator of the trust, and while he was sympathetic to my mother's situation, he was bound by the provisions of the trust. He comforted BB by saying that the bank was only interested in the interest on the loan, and they didn't care about repayment of the principal.

Financial salvation came when Mr. Adam Seiders, a tall, bald, retired tailor, rented Mr. Twyman's original upstairs apartment, my father's Social Security began to come in, and BB played the organ (for a small fee) at Hill and Irving Funeral Home several times each week.

Adam Seiders made his own suits and sport coats while he was a tailor and he was as well dressed as any man in Charlottesville. He retained the very heavy iron used in his tailoring business, and pressed his clothes each night in preparation for the next day. To have something to do, he went to work as a sales clerk in Nelson Brown's Gift Shop, a successful business in which he had also invested some funds to get the business started. Nelson Brown was so successful that he later bought the smaller mountain adjacent to Monticello and restored the old mansion which was on the top of the mountain.

While I knew that my family was not well off financially, BB generally shielded me from those problems and I really did not realize until later years how debt plagued we were. Had I fully understood the financial situation I would not have agreed to go away from home for my first year of college, my Father insisted that I get away from home and get on my own for at least a year. The basic plan always was that I would finish at "the University" (of Virginia).

BB told me several times that when she died, Hill and Irving Funeral Home would take care of her funeral. Well, they did. They conducted the funeral very nicely, but then they sent me the bill for everything. That is not what BB thought would happen, but I paid the bill without question, happy that BB would never know.

At Mimi's death, the house reverted to the Twyman Trust. The Bank was very kind to me about taking as much time as I needed to get all the furniture and other things out of the house but I was eager to get on with it so Martha and I went there for a week to get it all emptied and cleaned. We sold some things, gave away other things; but in that sad week we got it all done, and we essentially said good-bye to Charlottesville. We have been back there only a few times since.

One final comment about Horace Twyman. He always called me "Parson," suggesting that I would eventually enter the ministry. Many times in my presence, he explained to folks that I was an exceptionally good young man. In the presence of my elders, I only spoke if spoken to and then with sir or ma'am as appropriate. My parents trusted me, and I had never broken that trust. I did not cause any problems in school and was dedicated to attending Sunday School and church. Horace insisted that, with all those good qualities, it was very clear that I would end up as a minister, and he never called me anything but Parson.

In my senior year in high school, Mr. Twyman offered to fund my education at the Virginia Military Institute in Lexington, Virginia, but I declined that offer saying, "I am not interested in the military." More about that story later when I talk about my days as a Brigadier General.

Kindergarten and McGuffey School

My formal education started at age five in a kindergarten operated by Mrs. Doner on First Street, just a few houses off of High Street. The ground floor of her house had been opened up into several classrooms and she had a large fenced in back yard for our outdoor activities. I was an enthusiastic student and received lots of large gold stars on my monthly report cards. At the end of the school year I remember being very disappointed that after summer vacation I would not be going back there but would enter the first grade at McGuffey School, just a couple of blocks on the other side of High Street.

Two things impressed all six year olds when they started at McGuffey School: First, the large (for the early 1920's) red brick building, with large hallways and large staircases which went from the basement to the second floor. And second, the Principal, Miss Carrie Burnley, an old-fashioned lady who wore black taffeta, full-skirted dresses with a high neck collar and lots of lace at her neck and on the cuffs of her sleeves.

Miss Burnley could be a strict disciplinarian but she had a nice smile and was always very pleasant unless she needed to be otherwise. I liked going to school and starting in the first grade I always had a prominent role in every play and program that we put on for our parents. BB would tell me that she probably couldn't get there but she was always in the back, careful to stay out of my sight so as not to distract me or make me nervous.

My church experience prepared me to participate in school programs. I sang my first solo in Church at age four, dressed in a red velvet Lord Fauntleroy suit and was active in Church programs for the two years before going to McGuffey, so I was eager to participate in plays and programs and was always ready to take on a singing part. My Mother frequently served as the pianist for church services and my Father often sang in the choir, it was only natural that I was inclined towards singing and participating in church events. We did a lot of family singing at home, gathered around the piano while BB played. I can't remember a time when we didn't have a piano at home.

At age eight or nine, I started piano lessons with Mrs. Hill who lived up towards the University on Wertland Street. I had to walk there after school one afternoon each week and it was indeed a long walk. Further, after the lesson, I had to talk all the way home down to East Jefferson Street. It was about the same distance from McGuffey School to Mrs. Hill's as it was from McGuffey School to our home on East Jefferson Street. Walking was the accepted means of transportation in those days so it was not that I objected to walking, I objected to the long distances involved and the amount of time it took to walk those long distances.

Mrs. Hill was a fine teacher but she did little to make me want to play the piano. As a good music teacher, she wanted me to have the matter of scales, fingering and note counting that is absolutely essential to learning to play the piano or any musical instrument. Unfortunately, I found it all very boring and besides, all my friends were playing football, baseball, or some other games appropriate to the season of the year. Like many of my friends in older years, I regretted that I did not understand the need to master the fundamentals of music before moving on to performance levels and did not have the personal discipline to practice every day when there were so many other fun things to do with my friends.

In those days, everyone wore their best clothing to church, even down at the Junior Sunday School level. As I grew older, coat and tie was the routine outfit for Sundays. When I entered the University of Virginia all first year men (never called freshmen) wore men's fedora hats, coats and ties. In the second year, most of us discarded the hats but always wore coat and tie, the only exception being varsity football players who were allowed to wear their sweaters with "V" one day each week. With that experience behind me, it is no surprise that I always wear coat and tie to church and don't go along with the informal attire program (no tie, no coat) used in many churches in Florida in the hot summer months. My fundamental attitude has always been to let others do as they wish to do, and I will do as I wish to do.

In my last year at McGuffey School, I played on the football team. We played Venable School and a couple of other grade schools with nothing remarkable to remember about the program.

At the end of my final year at McGuffey, I received special recognition for never missing a single day of school during first grade through seventh grade. I was the only one so recognized for that achievement. Whether intended or not, by insuring that I went to school no matter what the weather was, or whether I felt like it or not, my parents bred an attitude in me that school was the most important event in my life at that time, and it was my responsibility to be there. Along the way, I found that on snowy days when very few of us showed up, we didn't have regular classes, played games with the teachers, and usually were allowed to go home early!

Since I walked a long way to get to school, I had extra time to be with my dog Fritz and play with other children on our street. Fritz deserves comment as an important part of my young life. Fritz was a brown and white Fox Terrier, strictly a mutt, which my family obtained from an unknown source. As an only child, I needed someone to talk to and Fritz was always available and was an attentive listener. He had big brown eyes and when I would talk with him, he fixed those brown eyes on mine and gave the appearance of understanding every word I said. When I had serious problems, Fritz and I would get under my bed or my parent's bed and talk things over. If I was crying about something, refuge under a bed was my way of dealing with the situation. Fritz knew I needed extra comforting in those situations and he would snuggle up to my armpit and share my misery with me.

While living on East Jefferson Street, down past Saint Anne's

School for Girls, Fritz did not show up for his dinner one evening. We went around the neighborhood calling his name, but to no avail. All of were very sad at the thought that we had lost him forever. Exactly one week later, BB was in an upstairs bedroom that led out on to an open porch with open stairs down to the ground when she heard a muffled bark that just had to be Fritz. She went out on the porch and looked around but saw nothing. While standing there she heard another weak, muffled bark. A week earlier, she had been going through an old high domed wooden trunk looking for an old quilt and the trunk was still sitting there. She lifted the top of the trunk and out jumped Fritz. He streaked down to the kitchen and drank from his water pan until we thought he would float away. How he survived for one week in that closed trunk defies all logic, but joy was restored to the family and, in particular, to me. We immediately went under my parents' bed to discuss his dark week in the trunk. His trunk experience was written up in the Daily Progress, and I deeply regret that I have not seen that clipping for many years.

Lane High School

Lane High School was located at the intersection of West Main Street and Ridge Street. An imposing old red brick building with all hardwood floors, it remains a sentimental favorite for all who attended there; but I understand that it has been demolished and replaced by apartment and office buildings.

The transition from grade school to high school was effortless despite a different location, primarily because the high school administrators were so well prepared to receive us. We all knew where to go and knew ahead of time who our homeroom teachers would be. The "home room" concept was new to us. We stayed the full school day in our assigned rooms at McGuffey, but now we were going to move to a different classroom almost every period, and it was the teachers' assigned rooms we had to learn. In addition, we had to learn the quickest route to get to the teachers' rooms and how to maneuver in the hallways when all the classes were changing at the same time.

The Principal was Mr. Hugh Sulfridge, six feet four inches tall, with gray hair and an imposing appearance as the man in charge. In charge of the office and chief administrator was Miss Virginia Bolling, a pleasant lady just over five feet tall, who had an amazing capacity to learn new students' names and which schools they had attended before coming to Lane. Once again, because I was such an extrovert and so involved in so many of the school activities, I worked very closely with both of them over my high school years and both of them influenced me favorably.

Miss Bolling taught me to kiss properly on stage. I had the lead male role in "Miss Blue Eyes," a musical comedy, and the female lead was Betty Shumate. Each of us had one or more solos and a duet, and the theme centered on our on-again, off-again romance. At the end of the play, a romantic embrace and kiss were necessary. One day after classes ended, Miss Bolling took us into an empty classroom, shut the door and said "Give Betty a kiss." As you would guess, Betty was embarrassed and so was I, but I moved in close and put my lips on hers, proceeding very lightly. Miss Bolling said, "No, no. It was clear that you didn't mean it. This time, be more forceful, make it last longer, and both of you turn your faces a little bit toward the back of the stage so the audience can better see your faces. Try again." And so we did try, several more times, until Miss Bolling finally said, "OK. We will work some more on that next week."

"Miss Blue Eyes" was a big success, and after the play, Betty and I took a lot of teasing from our friends about how our romance "looked so real." I decided I like acting: There were rewards attached!

Mr. Sulfridge made it his practice to walk around in the lunchroom at recess time. He often sat down at one of the lunch tables and just talked with the students, whatever they wanted to talk about. Early in my junior year, he sat down beside me one day and started the conversation by asking me what I wanted to do with my life. As a high school junior, I really hadn't given that topic a lot of deep thought. I responded by saying that the medical profession seemed to be real interesting and that I might be interested in the field of psychiatry. I clearly remember his response to my statement. He said that I should recognize that I would have to get a Bachelor's Degree, then go three or four years to medical school, and then a couple more years to specialize in psychiatry. "That is a lot of schooling before you can start practicing as a doctor, and those years of university training will be kind of expensive."

Obviously, I did not know how much schooling was required, and I certainly had not thought about the expense involved. I did not feel a deep sense of disappointment since my choice of possible profession had been an off the top of the head response to a question I had not expected.

He concluded his luncheon visit by saying that he knew it was very early for me to be making such a decision, but he wanted me to recognize that as I gave serious thought to what I wanted to do in the future, I should be sure I knew what I had to do to prepare for my chosen field, how much education it would require, and whether all of that would be financially feasible. His final statement was that he would always be available to me to provide information and advice. That little episode demonstrated what a fine Principal he was and how he earned the respect and admiration of his students.

My first two years at Lane produced no big memorable events. In my second year, I played on the junior varsity football team, which gave me a leg up in my junior year to play on the varsity team. Weighing in at 165 pounds, I played right tackle and was the ball holder (kicking tees were not allowed in those days) for kick-offs by Carl Barnett and ball holder for field goals.

Only two football games gave me memorable experiences. We played one game at Thanksgiving time in Scott Stadium at the University of Virginia. We played Hopewill (VA) High School, and their star running back was Josh Prichard, later a star at Virginia Military Institute over in Lexington. Josh was fast, ran hard with his knees up high, and was hard to tackle. I managed on a couple of plays to get through the defensive line and tackle Josh as he reached the line of scrimmage. Those couple of plays made my day and gave me good memories.

The other memory was a game against Alexandria High School in Alexandria in the first night game after lights were installed on their home field. Early in the third quarter, we punted and I took off down the field to tackle the receiver. About twenty yards before I got to him, I was hit by two blockers; one hit me high, the other hit me low and I was knocked out — completely unconscious. The next thing I remembered was being on a table in the Emergency Room of Alexandria Hospital. The doctors said I had no injuries and would be released when the team bus came by to pick me up after the game. What I remember so clearly was that I was running down the field, looking up into the lights to see the football, I was hit hard and all the lights (mine) went out. I did not remember being carried from the field, or the ambulance ride to the hospital. We were beaten by Alexandria High School, but not as badly as we had anticipated. They were in a different league from our small Charlottesville high school.

My junior and senior years at Lane High School were two years of great fun. I was doing well with my grades, was involved in virtually all school activities, had the lead role or a principal role in every theatrical production, and in my senior year was voted as "Lane's On–coming Best Actor." I was President of the Boys Glee Club and President of the Hi-Y Club and also served as President for the Central Virginia Hi-Y Clubs, an area which included Waynesboro, Staunton, and Lexington. I was a first team varsity football member and lettered in my junior and senior years. I was manager and trainer of the basketball team. As the trainer, I wrapped ankles and knees, and when we went on trips, I monitored food choices to insure that if a member chose fish, he did not drink milk with it and insured that no one chose too much desert.

The football and basketball coach was Harry Martin, a Charlottesville boy who had been a football star at the University of Virginia. I knew his family and he knew mine so we had a close relationship from the first day I reported for football practice. Harry had a mental breakdown in his forties and was confined to a nursing home for several years before his death. I visited him several times in the nursing home and it was always an emotional experience.

I formed the school's first orchestra (there was no band program in those days), consisting of piano (David Shepard), guitar (Ernest James), steel guitar (Jack Hodges), saxophone (Sam Cummings) and a couple of others. We played at several school assemblies and eventually ventured out into the local luncheon club circuit, Kiwanis and Exchange were our first engagements. I directed the orchestra and usually insured that I would sing a couple of songs. This orchestra had its limitations and, frankly, was not very good but we were enthusiastic and since we had the courage to give it a try, we were appreciated beyond our capabilities.

In my junior year, I started singing with local dance orchestras. The first orchestra I sang with was the Bus Smith Orchestra. Bus was an exceptionally professional guitar player who had played with Jimmy Dorsey and a couple of other big, nationally known bands at that time. As a young man he had suffered from polio and was left with a shorter, somewhat deformed right leg, so he limped rather badly when he walked. His condition made it difficult for him with all the travel on the big band circuit so he decided to come home to Charlottesville where he worked in a music store selling guitars, giving guitar lessons and, eventually, forming his own dance orchestra. He drew on student musicians from the University, municipal band members, and individual instrumentalists like Bruce Hanger, a fine trumpet player and operator of the municipal airport in Waynesboro, a small city just across Afton Mountain. While in the University, I took flying lessons from Bruce and after eight hours of instruction soloed and accumulated about ten solo hours before I went off to the Marine Corps. I was paying $7.50 an hour learning to fly and I enjoyed it but I had enough experience in that mode to know that I did not want to be an aviator in military service.

The Bus Smith Orchestra usually consisted of four saxophones (University students), two trumpets (Bruce Hangar and Bill Jenkins, local jeweler) piano (Ben Borden, an exceptional high school pianist), drums (Bernie Bolling, a house painter and heavy drinker), string bass (Harry James of the very musical James family) and rhythm guitar (Bus Smith). I fronted the band, waving a baton, singing and serving as announcer as required. The band members usually wore tuxedos and I wore a white coat with black bow tie. My pay was quite modest but the pay was the least of my concerns. I was doing a lot of singing, gaining a reputation, and meeting a lot of folks around the State. We played most weekends at Fry's Spring, a large dance hall operated by Mr. Russell Dettor who also operated (on the same property) the largest public swimming pool in the area.

In addition to having local social and civic organizations sponsor dances, Mr. Dettor needed to fill the dance hall calendar sometimes so I became one of his sponsors. I assumed the role of President of the

Eighteen Club. I was the only member but we would have invitations printed which read, "The President of the Eighteen Club invites you to attend a dance celebrating (for example) Saint Patrick's Day on (date)." He had a mailing list of younger folks (high school students, several nearby private schools) to whom we mailed the invitations and we always stated that the card was essential for admission. On the night of the dance, I would man the Cashier Window and collect the "Attendance Fee" as President of the Club. When the evening was over, we counted the cash, paid the orchestra (I was often part of that), withheld the cost of the invitations and postage, then Mr. Dettor and I split the remainder of the cash. The proceeds were not large but we always made something, and of course, he sold a lot of food and beverages, so he was always satisfied. I was happy to receive my share of the deal because gasoline

had gone up to twenty-three cents per gallon (up from twenty cents) and I needed a lot of fuel for my car.

Starting in my junior year, I always had a car to get to school, get to football practice, get around to collect my Father's business bills, and generally be a young man about town. My first car was a 1929 Ford convertible, dark green, two doors, a back seat, and a rumble seat. I gave that critter the name of "Agnes." My Father had acquired the car after a University student had a new convertible top put on and had leather upholstery custom made for all seats, including the rumble seat. The car was in great condition but the student decided to leave the University so he offered the car to my Father as payment for the bill he owed. What a great break for me! I was one of just a handful of students who drove cars to school in those days. We were allowed to park on the school grounds, and when the school day ended, I was out the door and in the car in less than two minutes. Having my own car and being very generous about offering rides to young ladies and to close friends, Agnes further enhanced my role as a BMOC (big man on campus). I did say earlier that my high school days were fun, fun, fun!

With my very busy slate of activities in my junior year, I let up on my involvement in the Boy Scout Troop. Fortunately for me I had a fine, dedicated Scoutmaster, a letter carrier of the United States Postal Service, Mr. Malcolm Campbell. I had completed most of the requirements for the rank of Eagle Scout and Mr. Campbell wanted me to achieve that rank because there weren't many Eagle Scouts in those days so he stayed after me to finish the job and I was awarded my Eagle Scout Badge in the Fall of 1937.

Some 26 years later, while serving as Vice President, Far East Council, Boy Scouts and Girl Scouts of America, I was awarded the rank of Distinguished Eagle Scout, honoring me for distinguished service in a number of different activities and for my continuing support of the Boy Scout program for more than 25 years after receiving the rank of Eagle Scout. I continue to display that plaque and wear the silver eagle insignia with great pride. In hindsight, I have to be grateful to Mr. Campbell for keeping my priorities straight at the right time in my high school experience.

In my senior year at Lane, the local radio station and several local merchants joined to sponsor an amateur hour competition, with the winner going to New York City to compete on the Major Bowe's Amateur Hour radio programs, one of the most popular radio programs across the nation. A lot of future stars in the musical world got their first national exposure on Major Bowe's program. There were a series of six competitions, with the six winners competing in the final program at the newly opened Paramount Theater, the first competition for the locally owned Twyman Brothers Theaters.

I won on the night of the preliminary competition and waited for the final competition to take place. Frankly, most of the competitors were not very good but I quickly identified who my major competitor would be. It was a pretty girl, three or four years older with lots of voice training, who specialized in light opera and light classical songs. She was very good and certainly was much more polished than I was. After three rounds of applause for each of us, the judges declared her the winner. She went to New York, appeared on the Major Bowes amateur program, performed very nicely but could not compete with those big city, "professional amateurs" from the Julliard School of Music and from other top-notch training schools. I would not have fared any better than she did, so in hindsight, I was happy that things turned out as they did.

That amateur competition led to the local radio station asking me to do a thirty minute, once a week radio program. The way we worked it out, the program was called "Larry presents Bus, Ben, and Harry." The announcer (Ed Hayes) would say "Larry presents Bus (Bus would do four or five measures of fancy fingering guitar chords), Ben (Ben would play three of four beautiful piano chords), and Harry (Harry would make a few fingering runs on the bass viol), and they would hit an agreed chord. Then the announcer would say, "Now here is Larry to sing '....'"

I usually did two songs, paused for a commercial, sang one more song and then the musical trio played a number; then another commercial, then two more songs by me; then a solo number by either Bus or Ben and then I closed out the program with one or two songs. The programs went very well and we never committed any major gaffes.

Three days after the first program, I received my first fan mail: a postal card from Mrs. C. C. Sours, requesting that I sing "Red Sails in the Sunset," which I did and I dedicated the song to her.

Stetson University

Despite the lean economic base of my family, my Father was dedicated to the idea that my first year of college should be away from my hometown. He was equally dedicated to the idea that I should graduate from "the University" (University of Virginia). In the summer of my junior year in high school, I began looking for a small college, reasonably priced, somewhere in the South, and known as a Baptist school.

Stetson University in Deland, Florida was recommended to me by a musician in a traveling orchestra playing for a dance in the old gymnasium at the University. I went to the dance just to listen to the dance band which had a good reputation for playing Glenn Miller style dance music. It was a first class orchestra. During one of the orchestra breaks, I introduced myself to the piano player and told him how much I enjoyed the music, told him I sang for a local dance orchestra and told him I was looking for a college to attend the next year. He assumed that I was interested in a good music school so he told me about Stetson. He said Stetson had a superb music department and was located in the very nice small town of Deland, Florida. So I wrote for the Stetson catalogue and it proved to be just what I was looking for and was not too expensive by comparison with other schools whose catalogues I had examined. I applied and was quickly notified of acceptance.

We began to get ready for departure by buying a small trunk and a suitcase and gave a lot of thought to my clothing needs. Mother and I went to Newman's Men's Clothing Store and bought me two suits; one was off-white with random deep blue vertical short stripes (for sunny

Florida) and the other was dark blue for church wear. Both suits turned out to be mistakes. We had been influenced by University of Virginia student apparel where students wore suits or some kind of coat and slacks and all "first year men" wore men's fedora hats. Arriving at Stetson I learned that freshmen wore little green beanies (small caps with small visor) and the only time to wear a suit was if you went downtown to the big Baptist Church, but not too many suits were to be seen even there.

At 10:00 each morning, we all attended Chapel Services for 30 minutes, sang a few old-time hymns, and listened to a short sermon. The class day was over by 3 pm, so there was a lot of time for intramural athletics and leisure time. Many times, we would hitchhike over to Daytona Beach, just 23 miles away, and most motorists were very kind to students thumbing a ride. I still have a scar along the inside of my left little finger from playing on the beach. Running from Joe Patillo, a dormitory friend from New York, who was chasing me with a jelly fish in hand, I ran around a car parked on the beach grabbed the license plate to keep from falling and cut my little finger open from top to bottom. I bled a lot and the finger looked awful, but a lifeguard bandaged it up and told me to get back to the student infirmary as quickly as I could. A doctor in the infirmary put in some stitches and taped up the hand and it was all right after about six weeks but the scar is still visible. All freshmen arrived ten days before the upper classmen in order to have daily orientation and after five days, the fraternities and the sororities were allowed to "rush" for new members. I was wined and dined by three fraternities and chose Sigma Nu. I remain a life member (and still get yearly appeals for money!).

Stetson was usually the first football game of the season for the University of Florida, just a warm-up game for the Gators. In 1938, the game was played in Gainesville and was a big game because it was the first night game under the lights in the UF stadium. Stetson was said to be the underdog by about 21 points but Stetson won the game 16-14 and the three hundred or so Stetson students who had gone up for the game were ecstatic. About a dozen or so of us Sigma Nu's went over to the UF

Sigma Nu house and partied until quite late. The next morning at an early hour, we drove over to Rollins College for a Stetson-Rollins Playday, a day of intramural games and sporting contests. I was on the swimming team and when I dove into Lake Virginia I thought I was in the Arctic Ocean, it was so cold. We won some and lost some but it was all friendly rivalry so nobody really cared whether we won or lost. I was impressed by the beauty of Rollins College and thought there were tons of pretty girls there. I vowed I would go back there but I never did. My grades at Stetson were not sparkling but they were good enough to gain my acceptance at the University of Virginia when I submitted my application to start my second year of college. Like most of the other freshmen at Stetson, I spent too much time having fun in extra-curricular activities and enjoying the sun and the beaches of Florida. I believe it was the growing-up experience my Father wanted it to be.

The University of Virginia

Because of my one year at Stetson University, I entered the University as a "second year man" which meant I was not required to wear a fedora hat but I used to wear one quite often anyway. I was more comfortable back in an environment in which I wore a tie and a coat to classes and somehow felt more mature because of those dress standards. It also gave me a more mature attitude about my studies and got me to thinking about what I wanted to do when I finished at the University. It was now moving into 1940 and the clouds of war were very heavy in Europe. Fortunately, I had a couple of professors who spent a few minutes on the world situation before we got to the topic of that class and later I realized how much they had prepared me to think about the possibility of war involvement by the United States.

At the end of my second year, I applied to the Marine Corps for a two-year summer program (Platoon Leaders Class). In that program, I would go to Quantico for six weeks for two summers and if successful, would be commissioned a second lieutenant in the Marine Corps Reserve upon graduation from the University and then go on active duty as needed. A form letter response from Headquarters Marine Corps informed me that the classes were already filled but I was provided with an application to become a Naval Aviator. I mistook that to mean that I would be in the Navy and that was not what I had in mind. At that time, I was paying seven dollars an hour learning to fly over at the airport in Waynesboro and already knew that flying was not my cup of tea. I had soloed a Piper Cub and had about five hours of solo time and knew that I wanted to fly when I wanted to fly and not when ordered to fly in less than pleasant flying weather.

An early action was to affiliate myself with the UVA chapter of Sigma Nu. I developed some good friendships there, attended Chapter meetings faithfully and dropped by the house a couple of times each week to play pool or ping pong and generally talk about matters of mutual interest with whoever was there at the time. The ten or twelve brothers who lived there and took their meals there got the most out of being in the fraternity. As a local student who lived at home and did not have the financial resources that most of the brothers had, I probably got less out of the fraternity relationship than any other member did. I enjoyed a beer or two on occasion but learned very early that drinking and driving did not mix well and my car ownership and my driving were too precious to risk.

I participated in baseball, basketball and boxing---not as a player but in an administrative role. For the boxing matches, which were tremendously popular in those days, I was the ring announcer to introduce the boxers and announce the winners to the audience of several thousand who packed the old gymnasium. During baseball season, I was the loudspeaker announcer to read off the line-ups and provide other information as the games went on. For varsity basketball I was Assistant Manager and for several lengthy periods of each season was the Manager because the designated Manager had to go home to northern Virginia for family reasons.

One of my great pleasures was to sing in the University Glee Club, in the tenor section of course, and sang first tenor in the Tin Can Quartet. I was joined by Ted Butterworth, second tenor, Ed Berry, baritone, and Joe Tucker, bass. The Tin Can Quartet was the most popular part of our Glee Club concerts and sometimes we performed on our own, separately from the Glee Club, and we were always a hit. We were blessed with a director, Howard Bailey, a reporter for the Daily Progress newspaper, who was very talented and who made us rehearse until we did it right and then rehearse some more.

The extra effort paid off. When the four of us were graduated as a part of the Class of 1942, the Director of the Glee Club, Dr. Harry Rogers Pratt, retired the idea of another Tin Can Quartet, saying publicly at our final concert that there would not be another group of four who could produce such close barbershop harmony. We were quite proud of that tribute.

After these many years and having reflected on my years at the University, I am ready to confess that I was overextended in my several activities and am not sure how I kept my grades at a satisfactory level, even attaining the Dean's List of Distinguished Students in the first semester of my senior year. I didn't get much sleep and that was a worry for my Mother who reminded me of that often but didn't nag me about it. Starting in my second year at the University I started singing with dance bands (the Bus Smith Orchestra, the Hartwell Clark Orchestra, and a few times with the Bruce Hanger Orchestra). On weekends and sometimes on a weeknight when we played for a dance or special program outside of town, I did not get home and in bed until 2 or 3 a.m. and usually had to get up for class or other activity early the next morning. I worked in the University Book Store the first five or six weeks of each new semester when the rush was on by students to buy and sell textbooks. As a shoe salesman, I worked lots of weekends at the Shoe Center downtown, was covertly slipping over Afton Mountain to Waynesboro to take flying lessons, was spending lots of rehearsal time with the Tin Can Quartet, was managing one of the several varsity athletic teams, announcing the boxing and baseball events, and lastly, but of great importance, I was spending a lot of time courting Miss Martha Ham, waiting lots of nights for the Standard Drug Store to close at ten 10 pm so I could drive her home. I knew I was doing too much and wasn't getting enough sleep or rest but I just didn't feel I could give up any of those activities. All this explains why, when I enlisted in the Marine Corps Reserve, I was described as being six feet tall and weighed one hundred sixty five pounds, the same weight I had four years earlier when I played left tackle on the Lane High School football team!

On Sunday afternoon, 7 December 1941, the Tin Can Quartet was rehearsing in Ed Berry's room on the Lawn and approximately four thirty, an excited student knocked loudly on the door and when Ed opened the door, the student said, "The Japanese have bombed Pearl

Harbor." A voice asked, "Where is Pearl Harbor?" Howard Bailey and I
simultaneously said, "Pearl Harbor is in Hawaii," and then Howard
added, "That means we are at war against Japan." We agreed to spend
another half hour in rehearsal and then go home to listen to the radio.

The next day, a half dozen of us headed downtown to the Post
Office where we knew the military recruiters were to be found. Three of
us went directly to the Marine desk. There was a rough looking older
Sergeant sitting there and he was quick to say, "You University boys will
have to wait for the Recruiting Officer to get here because he will want to
consider you for the officer programs." He took our names, home
addresses and phone numbers and said, "We will call you in a couple of
weeks."

In mid-January, the Recruiting Officer arrived, arranged for my
physical exam, obtained a transcript of my Stetson and UVA courses and
grades and gave me an appointment for his next visit scheduled for mid-
February. On 21 February, I was sworn in to the Marine Corps Reserve as
a Private First Class and was told to stay in school until I received orders
to active duty from Marine Corps Headquarters. Within the first few
days of April, the orders arrived, directing me to report to Quantico,
Virginia on 5 May to attend the 7th Candidates Class. My first action was
to have those orders in hand and visit with Dean Furgerson, to clarify
what affect my leaving in early May meant to my planned June
graduation. He said he would have to discuss it with the Faculty
Committee and then get back to me. Two days later his secretary called
and said the Dean had answers for me. I was in his office when he
arrived the next morning. He went right to the point. He said, "I
discussed your case with the Faculty Committee. They took note of the
fact that you are currently on the list of Distinguished Students, thought
you would do well on the comprehensive exams which are coming up
next week, so they agreed that you should report to Quantico as ordered.
We will read your name at graduation time and will mail your diploma
to you at Quantico. We wish you every success in your Marine Corps
service." Weak in the knees and almost overwhelmed by all the good
news, I thanked the Dean profusely and sped away home to tell my

parents the good news and then to let Martha know about my plans.

A day or two later, I stopped by the ATΩ fraternity with my good friend Roy Foulkrod and was invited to go to the attic to see six newly arrived Collie (mixed breed) puppies. Cute, like all puppies, I asked, "What are you going to do with all those puppies?" The Chapter President said, "Anybody who asks that question gets one. Which one do you want?"

By that time, one of the puppies had chosen me. A tri-color black, brown and a little bit of white had kept coming over to me and then walking away, his little hind end rocking from side to side as he walked away. He would only go about six feet away and then come running back to me. I said, "This is the puppy for me but I cannot take him until I talk with my parents. I will take him tomorrow if they agree." It was agreed they would hold him for me for 24 hours. My pitch to my parents was that he would be replacement for me while I was away in the Marine Corps, that I would be there to get him house broken, that I had already named him Rocky for the way he walked, and I just knew they would love him. There was very little discussion and they both said to "bring him home tomorrow," which I did. Within three days, Rocky learned that when he needed relief he should be outside with his feet on the grass. Later Rocky became a very modest dog and would always go behind a bush or a section of the hedge to relieve himself. He quickly became an important and dearly loved member of the family. Some pictures of Rocky are included herein.

On the morning of 5 May 1942, my parents, along with Uncle John (C&O City Ticket Agent), saw me off on the train headed for Washington, D.C. Even today, to get to Quantico by train from Charlottesville, you must go to Washington and change to a train headed to Richmond or go to Richmond and change to a train headed for Washington. Taking the Washington route allowed me to get to Quantico just after noontime. So we now turn to my years in the Corps.

World War II

In another volume is an Oral History Interview which was conducted by a Florida State University graduate student for the FSU Oral History Program and the Institute for World War II. That interview provides broad coverage of my World War II experience. In that narrative I do not deal with my personal battlefield experiences nor will I do that here. Suffice it to say that on the battlefields I did what I was sent there to do and did it to the best of my ability and training. I have no desire to relive the carnage of the battlefields except to note that I was exposed to a lot of it. I have no desire to paint myself as a combat hero because, like all my Marine associates, I was just doing my duty and I wanted no special recognition for that. I had the good fortune to survive my experiences in three wars and know how fortunate I was to escape with being just twice wounded and luckily those wounds were not crippling or disfiguring. I will limit this section to personal incidents which I remember pretty clearly.

Additionally, interested readers might read the oral interview about my Marine Corps career which was conducted by Bob Taglianetti, a representative of the History Division at Quantico. Taglianetti came to my home in Tallahassee where we spent four hours on each of three days in interviews. He had reviewed my entire record of service (fitness reports, medical records, and other material) and surprised me with how much he knew about my service. I was provided with a draft copy of his report to and invited to edit it for content to insure its accuracy. I did just that, so if errors are found, I am responsible.

To start at the beginning, why was I interested in the Marine

Corps? The simple answer is that my family dentist, Dr. Sims, baited me with the challenge that I probably was not tough enough to serve as a Marine, always ending on the note that the Corps would be too tough for me. He had served in Nicaragua, so I went to the World Book reference books to read about Marines in Nicaragua. No question about it, it was tough duty; but I didn't

see anything that said I couldn't do it. Every visit with him over my years

and into the University, his message and challenge to me were the same. Even before the Japanese struck Pearl Harbor, it was clear to me that if war came, it would be the Marine Corps for me. I was determined to prove to Dr. Sims that I was tough enough to be a Marine.

When the war ended and I went home, before going to my first duty station, I put on my uniform and went to call on Dr. Sims at his home. Mrs. Sims told me he died a year or so earlier, so I had no opportunity to say to him, "I told you I could do it." In the final analysis, I know it was the challenge from an Ol' Corps Marine that brought me to the Corps.

Marine Corps Base, Quantico, Virginia

Shortly after Noon on 5 May 1942, I stepped off the train on the platform at the Marine Corps Base, Quantico, Virginia. I believe I was the only passenger who got off the train at that point. Waiting for me was a tall, recruiting-poster Marine Sergeant, red faced, red hair, and with khaki shirt and trousers tailored to a perfect fit. He said, "Welcome to Quantico and to the Marine Corps," and with that simple greeting, I was in my new world, which was to become my universe for the next thirty-seven and a half years.

The Marine Sergeant escorted me to the Base Headquarters building and then to my barracks building, where he left me with a Corporal who would explain my schedule for the next two days as other Members of my Candidates Class were arriving. Mine was the 7th Candidates Class, and those of us who were successful and were commissioned would become the 10th Reserve Officers Class (10th ROC).

7th Candidates Class

Candidates Class was a boot camp for the mix of college graduates, some Marine Non-Commissioned Officers who had been recommended for commissioning, and a few Reservists who were seeking to become officers. Some of the college graduates had one or more years of ROTC training and were well ahead of the rest of us who were experiencing military routine for the very first time. Later on, and when I was in Officer Training, I was bound and determined to out-do some of them, and I did. There was not much to recount about my Candidates Class; it was just learning basic military language, incessant close order drilling, and doing everything on the double. It was physically challenging, but I made my first mark in the Corps when I won the obstacle course race and was given a ticket to see a USO show on the weekend in the Base Theater. The show featured Bob Hope and a gaggle of pretty showgirls.

I remember well the "purple shoe" incident. When I was sent to Supply to draw my first shoes and clothing items, I was looking forward to getting a pair of high-top cordovan shoes which most Marines were wearing at that time. When I stepped up to the window to draw my shoes, the Corporal there said there were no more cordovan shoes; I would be issued the new wartime field shoe, which was a non-glossy, lighter colored shoe. I would wear a low-quarter cordovan color shoe when they became available. What a let-down. Back at the barracks, one of my classmates was a Staff Sergeant who had been on recruiting duty. He said I could go to the Post Exchange and get some cordovan color shoe dye and then use cordovan polish on them and they would look just fine. I followed his advice and, after lights out at 10 pm, I went to the head, dyed my shoes, and returned to my bunk, proud of my work. The next morning we were to be inspected in our new uniforms. Leaving my shoes for last, I dressed and then reached for my shoes and was horrified to see they were purple. I had no alternative but to wear them.

The inspecting officer, Colonel E.O. Ames (later a Brigadier General), was led down the ranks by my Company Commander, Captain Gottshalk. When Colonel Ames came to me, he said, very softly, "Son, where did you get those purple shoes?" I told him what I had done in my effort to have cordovan shoes. With that, he turned to Captain Gottshalk and ripped about three layers off his back for allowing that to happen to me. Even at that point in my military career, I did not think it was a good idea for a Colonel to chastise a Captain in front of his troops. I was relieved that no punishment was suggested for me.

In July, I was commissioned a Second Lieutenant and moved to another barracks. I don't know how many of my Candidates Class members did not last long enough to be commissioned, but there were more than a few. Some of them reverted to enlisted rank, and a few were simply discharged and sent home.

10th Reserve Officers Class

The Commander of my ROC was Colonel Walter W. Wensinger, an Ol' Corps Marine who spent 17 years in the Marine Corps Band as a piccolo player. As a Colonel, Wensinger commanded the 23rd Marine Regiment when we landed on Iwo Jima and later, as Brigadier General, he was the Assistant Division Commander of the 4th Marine Division.

An imposing figure, he assembled us on the Barracks steps on our first Friday afternoon in ROC. He told us were being given liberty at 1600 and we did not have to start our training until Monday morning at 5:40. He said, as he called us "Gentlemen" for the first time, "Please remember that the Marine Corps does not run the buses, the railroads, or the trains. You may go anywhere you want to go for the next two days, but it is your responsibility to be at reveille on Monday morning. There will be no excuses. Enjoy your first liberty."

ROC training was tough, thorough, and physically demanding, with long days and long nights out in the Chopawamsic Creek area of the Quantico base. Just like in Candidates Class, we did almost everything on the run, always running up the barracks steps, where I

was on the third floor. When we completed ROC we were awarded
Certificates of Completion, and on the bottom of the Certificate were
listed the courses we had taken. A red line was drawn through
Administration because I did not pass that course. I could never
understand the Muster Roll system in effect at that time. So, what is
interesting about that? My first assignment after WWII was to Quantico
to attend Administration School for ten weeks, and after I was there for
five weeks I was told that I would be staying there as an Instructor! A
couple of weeks after that I was told to go up to Headquarters, Marine
Corps, for an interview – with no indication what the interview was for.
That story follows the end of this section relating to WWII.

Camp Lejeune, North Carolina

On the day of commissioning, I received orders to proceed to
Camp Lejeune, North Carolina, for duty with the 3rd Marine Division,
Fleet Marine Force. At 3rd MarDiv Hqs, I was sent on to the 23rd Marine
Regiment and from there to the 3rd Battalion and on to Company K,
where I was assigned as a Platoon Leader. This was the time of buildup
for the Regiment, so there were a number of officer positions vacant.
Within a month, I was Acting Company Commander for a few days, but
then Captain Frank Snepp arrived and I reverted to Platoon Leader. After
a few weeks, Snepp was moved to another billet and another Captain
arrived, as reassignments were the order of the day.

My Battalion Commander was LtCol John R. Lanigan, an Old
Corps Marine with many years in the Corps. On my third day as a
Platoon Leader, I was summoned to Colonel Lanigan's office (in a
cardboard hut) along with two other Second Lieutenants. He had us sit
in three chairs lined up in front of his desk. He then queried each of us
about our family background, our impressions of our Candidates Class
program, and our experiences in the Reserve Officers Class. He then gave
us a brief summary of his Marine Corps experience.

Then he delivered his message to us: "You officers have assumed
positions of great responsibility. Most of the young Marines under your

command are away from home for the first time in their lives. You are young but they are younger, so you are going to be the mama and poppa for your Marines while at the same time, you are training them for survival on the battle field."

With that said, he presented each of us with a pocket-sized notebook and then continued, "This is your platoon leader's notebook. In it you will record the family facts about each of your Marines. I expect you to know about their family members, what they did before coming into the Marine Corps, and what they want to do when the war ends. Above all, you must always remember that the Marines under your command are not there to serve you, you are there to serve them."

I did not realize it then, but I later understood that he was introducing us to the concept of "servant leadership." It was not called that in those days, but now there are schools and institutes which proclaim that they teach the concept of servant leadership. In my case, I took the lesson to heart and tried to lead my troops based on that concept of leadership. When I retired and went into an executive position in the corporate world, I based my actions on that same concept. It works!

When I joined the 23rd Marine Regiment it was a part of the 3rd Marine Division. Within a couple of months, we Platoon Leaders were told to make an A list and a B list, and we were cautioned to make them as equal as we could. That is, don't put all the best Marines on one list and the slowest trainees on the other list, because the Company Commander would assign us to one list or the other and we didn't want to end up with all the slow learners.

We soon learned that the 23rd Regiment would be split in half with one half remaining as the 23rd Marines; the other half would become the cadre of a new 25th Marine Regiment. I stayed with the 23rd Regiment, but that meant that I had a lot of friends over in the 25th Regiment. Later, after the 4th Marine Division was activated at Camp Pendleton, California, we were joined by the 24th Regiment, the 14th Regiment (artillery) and other units (Pioneers, Communications, Medical) to flesh out the new 4th Marine Division.

Camp Pendleton, Oceanside, California

Camp Pendleton was the newest Marine Corps Base and was formerly the Santa Margarita Ranch in Oceanside, California. There were no good maps for the Base, so some of our battalion-size exercises were almost laughable but we learned a lot about what not to do when you don't have good maps. In our first battalion in defense exercise, Colonel Lanigan used an Esso Gasoline Company road map. I was Acting Company Commander of K Company, and when he showed me the area my company was to occupy, his thumb was in San Clemente and his little finger was almost in San Diego. After he gave the Company Commanders his five-paragraph order and departed, we Company Commanders decided how we would basically follow his plan. When he came back to check us out, he said we did splendidly! We spent a lot of time fighting brush fires in the outer training areas – fires caused mainly by exploding ordnance (mortars, artillery, tracer bullets). Our emphasis was on learning to use our supporting units (like the pioneers and tanks) and coordinating with the other Regiments. By the time we sailed out of San Diego headed for our first combat at Roi and Namur Islands, we were a well trained outfit.

Roi and Namur Islands

We were the first American combat Division to sail directly from an embarkation port and go ashore on enemy territory. Roi and Namur were very small islands surrounded by coral atolls, but they were important in the sense that they provided our first combat experience, taught us a lot about the cunning of the Japanese soldiers, and impressed us with the value of camouflage. They were superb at hiding snipers in palm trees and in the use of spider holes and other hidden positions. Our dead and wounded brought us face to face with death and pain, and it made us more dedicated to serious training for whatever we would next face.

We went to Maui, one of the Hawaiian Islands, to establish our base camp, refurbish our equipment, and for more hard training. We did not know it then, but our next objectives would be Saipan and Tinian, much larger islands with a Chamorro civilian population, though not very large, that we would have to take into account.

4th MarDiv Base Camp, Maui, Hawaii

On Maui, our Base Camp was a tent camp where we had canvas cots, but they were most welcome after all the time we spent sleeping on the ground. We refurbished our equipment, received new utility uniforms, and settled in for some very intensive unit training. Our Camp was quite a way up Mount Haleakala and the scenery was beautiful. It was tent camp only for most of us, and the showers were outside and very cold water only. The native population loved having the Marines there, and many Marines got to visit in local homes and develop close friendships. Because I seldom went to

the little town of Wailuku, I did not develop such friendships. I only went to town to get laundry done and never just to go on liberty.

The West Loch Incident

When it was time to load up and head for our next amphibious operation, K Company was loaded aboard an LST (Landing Ship, Tank) and moved to Pearl Harbor where the amphibious task force was being assembled. One of the outer lying areas of Pearl Harbor was called the West Loch area, and a large number of our LSTs were anchored there, usually in clusters of five LSTs around a dock. On a Sunday afternoon at approximately 3 pm, an event took place which was carefully withheld from public knowledge and hopefully from the Japanese. Each LST was fully loaded and every available inch of deck space was used to store extra drums of gasoline, water cans and ammunition. One cluster away from my LST, mortar rounds were being transferred from the ship's elevator to a truck. Reportedly, a round was dropped and exploded. That in turn set off other explosions of ammo and fuel, and almost instantly, five LSTs were burning. Those explosions sent hot shrapnel and flaming debris on to other LSTs, but most of them were able to extinguish the fires before they got out of control. Other LSTs in the area tried to get underway so they could escape further damage.

There was lots of burning oil on the water, and a number of Marines and Sailors were in the water, having been blown overboard by the several explosions. In total six LSTs were burned and lost, and three others were badly damaged and were sunk. I believe it is a tribute to the amphibious capabilities of the Navy-Marine Corps team that replacement personnel and replacement LSTs were immediately brought in, and the reconstituted task force was only 24 hours delayed in departing West Loch for Saipan; that lost time was made up en route to Saipan. I believe the final count was 207 Marines killed in the West Loch incident.

Saipan Island

The landing on Saipan was heavily contested by the Japanese, and we took a lot of artillery and mortar rounds en route to the beaches. Generally, things went as planned. On the second day as my company (Kilo Company, 3rd Battalion, 23rd Marine Regiment) was moving inland in the village of Charon Kanoa, we came upon a pile of bodies, about twenty natives, men, women and children; all appeared to be dead. As I was passing by the pile of bodies, I heard the soft cry of a baby. It was a baby girl, clinging to the body of her dead mother. I handed off my weapon, reached in, and pulled her away from her mother's body. She was crying as I held her, and my thoughts went immediately to the young son I left at home as I went into war. I thanked God that we were fighting overseas and not back in the States, where this kind of incident could happen. I knew that, at our landing, a native Chomorro veterinarian had joined our Regimental Headquarters to assist us with our fight against the Japanese. I radioed back that I needed that native to help me with a surviving baby. He came to our location very quickly and took her from me. Years later, I told that story at a Seminar on Saipan during the 50th Anniversary of Freedom for Saipan, and that started a search for that baby (who now, if alive, would be a mature grown woman). But after a year of trying, the locals gave up the search. It was an experience I will never forget.

Both Saipan and Tinian had very large fields of sugar cane, and that meant it was a happy area for large green flies which just loved all that sugar. When we had a moment to eat our rations, it was a fight to see who could get food to his mouth before the flies landed on it. Many Marines unwillingly ate green flies because the flies were faster than their hands.

During the fighting on Saipan, a runner was sent from Battalion Headquarters to tell me that Headquarters Marine Corps had sent a message asking if I was interested in accepting a Commission in the regular Marine Corps; an immediate response was required from me. Much to the surprise of my fellow Marines who heard the question, I said, "Tell them yes." The runner said, "Aye, aye, Sir," and took off running to Battalion Command Post.

When the Saipan operation was completed, I took my Company aboard an LST so we could land on Tinian in LVTs (Landing Vehicle Tracked). It was just for overnight, but after the evening meal, the Skipper of the LST and the other Marine Officers aboard gathered in the small Officer's Mess Area, and I took the oath of office as an officer in the Regular Marine Corps. My fellow Marine Officers were still giving me a hard time about my decision to "go regular," but I accepted their kidding quite willingly because I had attained a goal that had been in my mind since I received my Commission as a Second Lieutenant.

Tinian Island

On Tinian, we landed on a very narrow, rocky beach which had virtually no sand beach; but we surprised the Japanese defenders, and that is why that entry point was chosen. When I looked at that beach years later, I wondered how we did it; but we did it, and that's all that mattered at that time.

The Tinian operation was not a simple piece of cake, but it was another comparatively large island with lots of sugar cane fields, many of which had been burned away by aerial bombs, naval gunfire, and artillery rounds. Tinian was only a short distance over water from Saipan, so we had some artillery support from Saipan in the initial phase of the Tinian operation. When we left Tinian, we returned to our Base Camp on Maui to get ready for the next target, whatever it may be.

From a review of my Fitness Reports after my retirement, I learned that the Battalion Commander had recommended me for the Legion of Merit Medal based on my performance on Tinian. It was disapproved somewhere up the chain but I am not sure where. It matters not, but the fact is that, in those days, the Marine Corps did not award the Legion of Merit to officers below the rank of Colonel. I would have appreciated it if the award had been downgraded to a Bronze Star (which I know happened in one case in the 23rd Regiment) instead of simply disapproved.

A Walk With Stephen Ambrose, Historian

An esteemed historian and biographer of folks like President Eisenhower, Stephen Ambrose, along with his son and his wife, went on the Reunion of Honor trip a few years ago. He wanted to see the airfields on Tinian and the site of the loading and takeoff of the Enola Gay, the B-29 which dropped the first atomic bomb on Japan. I was the only member of the travel group who had served on Tinian, so he asked me to escort him around the island so he could gain an appreciation of the importance of that island.

We started by going to the narrow, rocky beach where I landed, where I described how we surprised the Japanese defenders and discussed the problems associated with the sugar cane fields and the smoke which came from their burning. We continued around the island, winding up on the North Field runway where the Enola Gay loaded on the bombs and departed for the main island of Japan, where the targeted cities of Hiroshima and Nagasaki were located.

We drove up to the two holes where the bombs awaited loading onto the aircraft. I pointed out the bombs were so heavy that they could not get taken out to the aircraft; instead, the aircraft drove up past the pits, did a 180-degree turn, and drove back to position the bomb racks immediately over the pits where the bombs could be lifted up onto the bomb racks.

I suggested that Ambrose read the bronze plaque which had been erected to identify the bomb loading pits, and we stood silent while he read the plaque, not once but twice, before he looked up and, looking at me straight in my eyes, said, "General, it just may be that these were the most important holes dug in World War II." My only response was a tepid, "You may be right, sir."

We returned to Saipan to rejoin the travel group, but I have the pleasant memory of spending an afternoon with a noted historian whose writings made history come alive.

Workman Island (Code Name for Iwo Jima)

Our next target was Iwo Jima, which turned out to be an iconic battle of the Pacific Ocean theater and all of WWII. Iwo Jima was the bloodiest battle in the Pacific Ocean Area and probably in our national history of war. I cannot adequately describe the carnage, the killings, and the heroism which took place on that nondescript little island, and there is little need to. The battle on Iwo Jima has been written about in countless number of magazine articles, books, film documentaries, and movies, and I can't add anything to all of that coverage. I will limit my remarks about Iwo Jima to the two times I was wounded.

We were fighting at the base of Hill 362A, an area which was being heavily defended by the Japanese. The Japanese had a large (362mm) rocket which was launched from a set of wooden rails, and when the missile was launched, it made a screaming noise which could be heard over almost the entire island. When we heard the launch, we would look in the direction of the launch site and could often get our sights on the missile in the air because it was so large and it looked like a forty-gallon trash can as it tumbled in its trajectory. We would hold up a finger, line up with the missile, and if it stayed on line with the finger it meant it was headed my way and that I should move left or right, whatever was feasible at the time. If the missile moved to the left or fight of my finger, we assumed that it was going somewhere else.

There is a saying on the battlefield that you never hear the round that gets you and that was my experience. I heard the screech of the missile launch, but I could not pick up the sighting. The next and last thing I heard was the explosion of the missile when it landed in my vicinity. The next thing I remembered, I was on a stretcher on the beach and someone offered me a cigarette. He told me I was being evacuated to a hospital ship as soon as a boat could be found to take me there. My hands were heavily bandaged and so was my head, but morphine or some other medication was keeping the pain down.

I was taken by some type of boat to the USS Good Samaritan, one of several hospital ships supporting the campaign, and had an overnight trip to Guam to Fleet Hospital 115. During the overnight trip, a couple of Navy nurses cleaned me up and gave me some sleep medication, and the next thing I remembered was being moved from a stretcher to a hospital bed and a doctor was removing my bandages. He said, "You are a very lucky Marine. You were a bloody mess, but the shell fragments were small and the back of your neck and your hands will recover very nicely. The nurse will bring you a mirror so you can see the back of your neck. You will see why I say you were lucky. I'll check on you this afternoon." And away he went.

Elsewhere in this tome there is a piece entitled, "Small, small world," which describes the remarkable string of people I met during my Hospital Ship/Fleet Hospital experience, starting with the first nurse who interviewed me when I was lucid during the overnight trip to Guam, so I will not repeat that here.

When the doctor returned in the afternoon, I told him that, since I was not seriously wounded, I wanted to back to Iwo and rejoin my Company. He said that it was his understanding that no wounded would be returned to Iwo. He further said that there was an Advance Headquarters of Fleet Marine Force just little ways down the road from the hospital, and he would give me a liberty pass if I wanted to go talk with them. I took the pass, walked out of the hospital, and hailed the first jeep that came along, which took me to the Advanced Headquarters. When I entered the building, the first person I saw was Captain Ron Spencer, an officer school classmate who was the Adjutant. I told him what I wanted, and he told me that no one was being sent back, but he would get me in to see Colonel James, Commander of the Advanced Headquarters, so I could make my request.

As I was about to enter Colonel James' office, in walked Captain John Alden, an artillery officer from the 14th Marine (Artillery) Regiment, 4thMarDiv, who had been slightly wounded and evacuated just as I had. He said he was there to request transportation back to Iwo Jima. So, he and I went in to see Colonel James together.

Colonel James was an Ol' Corps Marine who looked tough but could not have been kinder to two young junior Marine Officers. He queried us about our time on Iwo Jima before we were wounded and asked us why we wanted to go back to all that intense fighting. I was the first to speak.

I told Colonel James that I was a bloody mess when I left Iwo Jima, but my wounds were not serious and I wanted to return to my company. I told him that the Marines in the 23rd Marine Regiment had been my family for the past year or so, and at this time they were even closer than my wife and son, who were back in Virginia waiting for my return. I insisted that I was not a hero and was not seeking hero status; I just wanted to get back to my Marine family. I said that I felt a little bit guilty being safe here on Guam while my good buddies were still risking their lives 24 hours a day. I concluded by saying, "Sir, my request to you is that you permit me to return to Iwo Jima by the first available transportation."

In different words but following my theme, Captain John Alden made the same request.

Colonel James said, "Current policy is that we do not return any wounded to Iwo. But, I don't expect to get many requests like yours, so I will make you two exceptions to that policy. We have a plane leaving early in the morning, carrying blood plasma and the first mail to Iwo. It is cargo only, but if the pilot will let you on that plane, I will allow you to go back. I will have a jeep take you down to the airfield so you can find the pilot and see if he is willing to have you on the plane."

Thanking him profusely, we took off for the airfield and, with a minimum effort, we located the pilot. He warned us that there were no seats, we would have to sit or lie down on the bags of mail, and that it would be a cold ride, but he would be sure that each of us had a Marine Corps blanket. We accepted all of that with thanks for his willingness to take us, and we assured him we would sleep at the airfield so we would be ready to go whenever he was ready.

When we returned to Iwo Jima, John Alden and I made our way back to the 4th Division Headquarters. From there, we were sent on down to our Regiments, to Battalion, and I went back to my Company. During my first night back, a nearby explosion wiped out my hearing, and I was sent back to the Regimental Aid Station for treatment. I stayed there overnight, and the next afternoon, I went back to my Company and stayed with the Company until hostilities ceased on 26 March.

While I was overnight in the Regimental Aid Station, the 2nd Battalion was engaged in one of the best organized Japanese attacks of the campaign. LtCol Ed Dillon, the Regimental Executive Officer, came down to take over the Battalion when the Battalion Commander was wounded. The Battalion killed a large number of the attackers, and a number of the Company were wounded or killed, but the Battalion was victorious. Colonel Dillon received the Navy Cross for his actions during that fierce battle. I can only guess that

God had his own way of protecting me by not letting me be there for that ferocious battle.

Within a couple of days after 26 March, my Company loaded

aboard the USS Jean LaFitte, a Merchant Marine ship with civilian crew, for the trip back to Maui to our Base Camp to start training for whatever operation might be next.

Back to Base Camp on Maui

Once again, we went to work refurbishing our equipment, discarding our worn out utility uniforms, and getting ready for more intensive training. Immediate rumors were that our next operation would be against Mainland Japan, and that the 4th Division would be in Reserve because we had been in the assault for four major amphibious operations. We also heard that our Division would be required to send some of our combat-experienced officers out to the 3rd Marine Division on Guam, because the 3rd Division would be in the assault for the next operation and they had a shortage of officers.

One morning, the Battalion Commander called Captain Gus Grussendorf and me into his office. Gus was Company Commander, G Company. He and I were the only two Captains left in the Battalion. The Battalion Commander, Major Bob Davidson, said, "Headquarters Marine Corps has ordered this Division to transfer 30 combat-experienced Captains and Majors to the 3rd Division on Guam, because that Division will be in assault in the next operation while the 4th Division will be in reserve. This Battalion must provide one Captain. Which one of you will volunteer for transfer?"

Gus and I both stood mute. The Battalion Commander said, "I am not going to make that decision. I will let fate decide." With that, he took out a quarter, flipped it, and said, "Gus, you are heads." The coin came up tails, so he said to me, "You will be on an Army Channel Steamer tomorrow morning headed for Honolulu, where you will go by air to Guam. Good luck." So, after all I had been through with my fellow Marines of Kilo Company, my family for so many months and so many shared experiences, it was time to move to a

new unit and a new family. Fate made that decision, so there was no appeal and no one to cry to; just get packed and get going, a hallmark of Marine life.

Guam and the 3rd Marine Division

Arriving on Guam, I was transported directly to Headquarters, 3rd Marine Division and told I would be assigned as Company Commander, Easy Company, 2nd Battalion, 3rd Marine Regiment. I arrived at my new Company just at dinnertime. The next day, I was out in the field on a battalion-size defense exercise in command of my new company. Before that three-day exercise was completed, my battalion commander was relieved of his duties because he did not order us to move fast enough into the defensive position and because his own battalion command post was so badly camouflaged.

The Division Commander was Major General Graves B. Erskine, a commander who had a reputation for relieving battalion and regimental commanders frequently. My Regimental Commander made a disparaging remark about "baby-faced" young Army Air Corps Generals flying bombing missions over Japan. General Erskine arranged for my Regimental Commander to fly in a gunner's seat on one of those bombing missions over Japan so he would have a better appreciation of the dangers associated with those missions.

In August, the atomic bombs hit Nagasaki and Hiroshima, and the Japanese surrendered. When that happened, we were issued an extra ration of beer, and most of us stayed up all night as we celebrated the end of the war and speculated about when we would get to go home. Within a few days we had instructions from HQMC about how to calculate points for overseas service. Those with the most points would go home first. There was a catch for me, however; Reserve officers had first priority, and since I was a Regular Officer, I could not plan to go home very soon. I was then told that my Rifle Company would go to Chi Chi Jima to disarm the Japanese garrison there. So we painted our helmets white, stenciled on military police insignia, shined our combat boots, and prepared to go aboard an LST for the trip to Chi Chi Jima.

Three days before embarkation, we received new rules about the point system. Priority was given for those who had two or more Purple Heart Medals. I had two such medals for the wounds incurred on Iwo Jima, so I was pulled off the Chi Chi Jima assignment.

Available and eligible to return to the United States, Colonel Jim Tinsley, the Commander of the 9th Marine Regiment, requested my assignment, so I became the Regimental Adjutant. The regimental colors were to be returned to Camp Pendleton and the Regiment was to be decommissioned. For the purposes of going home, the Regiment was no longer a tactical unit but a collection of officers and enlisted men who were eligible to go home. So we embarked on a Merchant Marine ship and returned to San Diego and on up to Camp Pendleton, arriving there in early December.

The task for Colonel Tinsley and me was to get all those Marines home by Christmas – all except the two of us. We were the last two members of the Regiment, and our job was to write the closing chapter of the Regiment's history and then turn in the regimental colors. We managed to get that done in the week between Christmas and New Year's, and then I was free to head for Charlottesville for a few days' leave and then on to my next duty station.

During that holiday time, Colonel Tinsley and his wife Mary treated me as family, and I spent more time with them and their children in their home in Del Mar than I did on Base. Later on, we became very close friends and, much later, if I had not been selected for Brigadier General, I would have gone to work for him in a large corporation in Cincinnati, Ohio.

World War II ended for me when I flew into Washington, DC. There I met Martha and we took the train home, and I connected with son John Stephen, who did not know me at all because of my absence at war. My first night at home, Martha and Steve were in bed and I had sat up still talking with my parents. When I got into bed, Steve did not know who this stranger was getting into his bed, so he scrambled out of bed and headed downstairs, looking for BB (my mother) for safe refuge.

Between WWII and Korea

After home leave, my orders directed me to report to Marine Corps Base, Camp Lejeune, for further assignment. With Martha and Steve on board, I reported in at Base Headquarters and was told that we could stay in temporary officer quarters for five days, and that no decision had been made about my specific assignment. Just two days later, I was notified that my orders had been changed, and that I must proceed to Marine Corps Base, Quantico, Virginia, to attend the administrative school for ten weeks. We drove to Quantico, and two days later, started to the school. After five weeks in the course, Major Hilton, Director of the school, called me in to his office to tell me that I had been chosen to stay at the school as an instructor, that he had arranged for me to be placed on the base housing list as of the day I arrived in Quantico.

Base Housing included Midway Village, a collection of prefabricated cardboard huts with tin roofs in an area just south of the base, just off Highway 1. Within a few days, Martha, Steve, and I moved in to Midway Village. Just a week after that, I was called into the Major's office and told that, on the next day, I must go up to HQMC to meet with a Lt. Colonel Wermuth, reason unknown.

I arrived at HQMC during the noon hour and went directly to the G-4 section of Plans and Policies on the second floor of the first wing of the Navy Annex Building, which housed all of HQMC at that time. When I arrived in the section area, I noted that there were no individual office partitions, and I could quickly see that all the desks were empty, except one. At that desk sat a Marine Colonel reading a newspaper. He quickly spoke up and said, "Captain, all the workers are at lunch, but maybe I can help you."

I said, "Sir, I am here to see LTCOL Wermuth, but I am not sure why."

Pointing to an empty chair by the side of his desk, he said, "Sit down here and I will tell you why you are here."

When I was seated, he continued, "I am David Shoup, and I head up the G-4 section. You are being ordered up here for duty in this section, and LTCOL Wermuth will be your boss. He is a fine officer, and I am sure you will like working with him. We want to get you up here as soon as feasible, but Colonel Wermuth will discuss those details with you."

I said, "Sir, I am rather perplexed by this news. I was just told that I would be staying at the administrative school as an instructor, and I have just moved in to Midway Island Housing. And further, Sir, I don't have any experience in the supply area."

Colonel Shoup said, "First of all, let me explain what we do here and explain the difference between Supply and Logistics." With that, he gave me a short course in Logistics, pointing out that Supply is just one part of Logistics, which embraces all the areas of material support for the troops. He said, "General Supply is just one of the sections here. We have Ordnance Section, Communications Section, Equipment Allowance Section, Engineering Section, and you and colonel Wermuth will be the Logistics Section, which helps me tie all those sections together and, in coordination with all the other G sections of Plans and Policies, we recommend courses of action to the Commandant. As regards your change of orders, as we draw down from our wartime strength, there will be lots of sudden changes as we settle down to whatever we are going to be in peacetime. Housing is extremely difficult to find in this area, so you may have to drive from Midway Island every day until you can find something. You will not get a parking space inside the fenced area, but if you get here early, you can find a place out on the street. Just in time, here is Jack Wermuth."

Colonel Shoup said, "Here is your new boss. Welcome to Headquarters Marine Corps." With that, Colonel Wermuth introduced himself and said, "We want you to finish Administrative School, but get here as quickly as you can after that."

Two days after finishing Administrative School, I reported to HQMC for my first of several tours at that headquarters.

Headquarters, U.S. Marine Corps, 1946-1949

Little did I have any thoughts about it at the time, but in my later years, I realized that I had the good fortune to join the G-4 Section, which provided a number of general officers in the future. Colonel Shoup became Commandant; Colonel Fred Weiseman became a lieutenant general and commanded Quantico; Lieutenant Colonel Randolf McCall Tompkins became a major general; Major Lou Metzger became a lieutenant general; Lieutenant Colonel Butch Sanders became a brigadier general and commanded the Marine Corps Logistics Center, Albany, Georgia; Colonel Joe Tschirgi became a brigadier general and retired at that rank. I completed that group of "comers" by getting to be a lieutenant general.

During that first tour of duty at HQMC, I also worked closely with two other officers who became commandants. Colonel Wallace M. Greene was OP-O9M, the Marine Corps officer on the staff of the Chief of Naval Operations, and later commandant. Lieutenant Colonel Leonard Chapman was in the G-3 Section of Plans and Policies, and I worked closely with him on a number of day-to-day projects. He too was later Commandant.

Working with associates of that quality provided a super experience for me as a young captain. But even better was the relationship which I developed with Colonel Shoup. LTCOL Jack Wermuth and I constituted the Logistics Section of the G-4 Section. Our desks were face to face, and only about four feet from Colonel Shoup's desk. Every paper which went to Colonel Shoup came first to Colonel Wermuth and me, and that put us in the position of working very closely with Colonel Shoup every day. The working relationship I developed with Colonel Shoup gave me some advantage when I worked for him later, when he was the Commandant and I was the Joint Action Officer as a Lieutenant Colonel, in the G-3 Section under then Colonel Cushman, who later became Commandant.

In 1946, hearings were underway for the National Security Act of 1947, which defined the roles and missions for each of the services and established the United States Air Force, previously the Army Air Corps during WWII. The Commandant and a number of other generals and colonels were on Capitol Hill almost daily for congressional hearings related to the forthcoming legislation. While I had no part in those hearings and preparing papers for our witnesses, I had the benefit of reading the daily testimony of those who testified.

The Army was openly trying to eliminate the Marine Corps, saying that there is no future for amphibious operations and our ground troops should be assigned to the Army and our aviation elements assigned to the new Air Force. In the end, the Marine Corps was written into the act with an organization of three divisions, three aircraft wings, provision for a reserve, and appropriate headquarters organizations. The Commandant was not made a member of the Joint Chiefs of Staff, an action that was not taken until General Lou Wilson was Commandant in 1977.

Exposed to all that testimony and the Marines who were testifying provided a great education for me when I served in higher staff billets, because the attacks on the Marine Corps have been frequent and constant over the years. Starting as a captain under Colonel Shoup, I became one of the Corps' first Joint Action Officers as the Defense Department began its efforts to pull the services together to clean up after WWII and starting to implement the new National Security Act. I frequently attended meetings in the Pentagon, where I was the only Captain-level officer present and the other service representatives were colonels or higher. Colonel Shoup understood my concerns, but reminded me that I represented the Commandant and I should not be bothered by all those higher ranks. I took him at his word and stood tall when I expressed the

Marine Corps' point of view. It was another exceptional training situation for me. Later, when General Shoup was the Commandant, there were several instances in which he sent a proposed joint action to me for review (as a Lieutenant Colonel), even thought the routing sheet had Colonel Cushman's initials on it for approval but did not include my initials.

One of my favorite incidents with General Shoup happened a number of years later when I was a Lieutenant Colonel in the G-3 and was briefing him before he attended a Joint Chiefs of Staff meeting. There were five JCS agenda topics for that day, and I was the Marine Corps Action Officer on all five items. After briefing the Commandant on the first four items, I said, "Sir,
I am not completely ready to brief this last item. It is not of great interest to the Marine Corps, and further, I have not been able to determine the positions of the Navy and the Air Force on this item."

There was a dead silence in the room for a moment. No action officer had admitted to the Commandant that he was not ready for a complete briefing on a JCS agenda topic. General Shoup looked straight at me and said, "I appreciate your being so straightforward. I don't think it will be a major issue." He paused and then said, "Do you know how I got to be the Commandant?"

I said, "No, Sir. How did you get to be the Commandant?"

He said, "By doing one thing at a time."

I said, "Thank you, Sir. In this case, I simply ran out of time."

Following the briefing, Major General Jim Masters walked with me back to my office and sat down by my desk. He said, "How do you get away with talking to the Commandant the way you do? I don't think there is a general officer in this building who would have done what you did today, and if he did, he wouldn't get away with it."

My response was, "I don't think I was disrespectful in any way. I thought it was better to admit I wasn't ready than to pretend I was ready and be unable to answer questions if he had any. When I worked for

Colonel Shoup back in 1946, I learned that you cannot be anything but resolute when he challenges you, and if you give the appearance of weakness or being intimidated, he will push you even harder. I hope I will never have to do again what I did this morning."

As he left my office, General Masters turned and said, "Keep up your good work and you will have a bright future."

I will never forget that experience with General Shoup or that encouraging experience with General Masters, who remained one of my strong supporters.

The Korean War

When I arrived in Korea and reported in to Headquarters, 1st MarDiv, I was told that two Regimental Commanders had requested my assignment – Colonel Glenn Funk, Commander, 7th Marine Regiment, and Colonel Harvey Tschirgi, Commander, 5th Marine Regiment – and that the Chief of Staff of the Division would make the decision about my assignment. I had worked in the G-4 Section of Plans and Policies at HQMC with both of those colonels, and I had a good relationship with both of them. I didn't know who I would choose, but it was not my choice. That evening, I was asked to go to the Office of Colonel Bill Van Rizen (later a Lieutenant General and Chief of Staff at HQMC).

I had known him briefly at Quantico while I was in the Development Center and he was in Base Headquarters. He said he just wanted to say hello, renew our acquaintance, and tell me he had decided to assign me to the 7th Marines because Colonel Funk needed an S-4, Logistics Officer and I had the right background for that; and so it was!

My first job in Korea was as the S-4, Logistics Officer for the 7th Marine Regiment. On several occasions, I told Colonel Funk of my desire to get to one of the Battalions, and after four months, he allowed me to go to the 1st Battalion as the Executive Officer for the Battalion. My CO was LtCol Hal Thorpe, a Reservist from California and a super Marine. When we first sat together to get to know each other, he explained that it was his policy to visit the rifle companies up front every day and if he couldn't go, I would go; and that is the way we worked it. After five months in that job, I was moved to the G-4 Section of the Division Staff at the request of Colonel Earl Sneeringer, with whom I had worked in

HQMC in 1947-48.

While I was serving in the G-4 Section, the Armistice Agreement was signed to end the fighting. A demilitarized zone (DMZ) was agreed upon, and each side had to clean up their half of the zone to remove unexploded ordnance and any areas of debris which could interfere with clear vision all across the DMZ. For reasons unknown to me, I was designated as the Officer in Charge of the DMZ cleanup. Of course, I worked under the direction of Colonel Sneeringer and with the Division Chief of Staff, Brigadier General Jack Juhan. Juhan rode close herd on us each day, as he had been directed to do by the Division Commander, Major General Pate, later Commandant.

When that job was completed, it just happened to be my time to go home. The night before my departure from Korea, I was invited to have dinner in General Pate's Mess. After dinner, General Pate pinned the Legion of Merit on me, certainly a great surprise to me. Later, Colonel Juhan told me that as Chief of Staff he had told General Pate that as a matter of Marine Corps policy, the Legion of Merit was not awarded to officers below the rank of Colonel. General Pate allegedly said that he knew that but that I had done such a fine job on the DMZ cleanup that he was going to award that medal to me.

The rest of the story about that first Legion of Merit is that when I reported to the 1st Marine Corps Recruiting District in Boston (en route to be Officer in Charge of the Recruiting Station in New York City), I was in full khaki uniform and wearing the ribbons for awards and service in WWII.

The Colonel in charge of the District Office received me in his office, did not start by saying hello or welcome to the 1st District. He started by asking, "Major why are you wearing that Legion of Merit ribbon? The Marine Corps does not award that medal to Majors!"

My response was "Sir, General Pate pinned that award on me the night before I left Korea, and a copy of the citation is with my orders which I handed to the Adjutant when I came in." He said, "I will look at it. I will brief you this afternoon about what I expect from you in the

New York Recruiting Station. You may go."

Despite that very cold start, we got along all right while he remained as Director of the District, but I was not unhappy when he went to another duty station.

Marine Corps Recruiting Station, New York City

My office in the Recruiting Station was at 346 Broadway in lower Manhattan, just a stone's throw from the New York Stock Exchange and a very crowded, busy part of the City. Martha and I, along with our sons Steve and Brian, lived over across the Hudson River in Englewood, New Jersey with Martha's Aunt Evelyn (sister of Martha's mother). Aunt Evelyn Gulnak was a long-time widow and was a Master Pattern Maker for one of the leading dress designers in New York. Aunt Evelyn got up each morning promptly at 5 a.m., squeezed fresh orange juice, and ground coffee beans for her two cups of coffee. Then she caught the bus over to 179th Street, where she switched to the subway to go to her office in midtown Manhattan. While living with her as we waited to get into an apartment, I followed her same morning routine. I caught a bus at 5:40 a.m. to get to the subway at 179th Street, went all the way down to Canal Street, and walked about three blocks to my office. A tough daily grind, but I did what had to be done.

I had 14 million people in my recruiting area, which extended from the east tip of Long Island over into New Jersey, south to nearly Atlantic City and up north just short of Albany, NY. I had 14 Recruiting Substations around the area, including the very famous one in the middle of Times Square. I don't recall how many Marines I had under my command, but there were a lot of them, and all of them were Sergeants and above and some had twenty or more years of service.

As a norm, my station was expected to put in about ten percent of each new Boot Camp session at Parris Island, and we never missed getting our quota during my two years there. One month, we attained 145% of our quota, and I received a special letter from the Head of the Recruiting Branch in HQMC. I attached a copy of that letter to the Service Record of each Marine in the Station, and after a Saturday morning meeting of all recruiters, I hosted a luncheon at my own personal expense – I had no Marine Corps funds for such a luncheon – at a nice Italian restaurant just around the corner from the Station.

I had a lot of help from Reservists and others who had served in the Corps and were doing well financially in the commercial world of the big City. One Reservist was Vince Sardi, Jr., son of the elder Vince Sardi of restaurant fame. Vince Jr. was a Captain in the Reserves and did two weeks of active duty at the Station each Summer I was there. In between times, he visited the Station often and was most helpful when I needed a special contact for publicity purposes.

Another great helper was Colonel Ray Henri, an artist and poet and in close contact with important people in the City. Another Reservist was Colonel Bob Krindler, one of three brothers who owned the "21 Club," one of the most famous dining and celebrity meeting places in the City. All three brothers were great supporters of the military services, and the 21 Club was decorated like a military museum. Bob was the most active in military circles as a Reservist, and Marine Corps pictures and artifacts stood out among all the military items on display. Any time I went there in uniform, I was treated royally and never paid for a drink; I did not abuse that privilege.

While I had the Station, there was the unfortunate incident at Parris Island known as the Ribbon Creek Disaster. A Drill Instructor took a platoon of recruits out into the wetlands of Parris Island after dark, and they were caught up in a very fast incoming tide as they sought to cross Ribbon Creek. Several recruits died and several others were injured. About half of those involved had come into the Corps through my Station. That meant, among other things, that the incident would get front-page attention in all the newspapers in New York, and it did. One of the recruits involved, but not injured, was the son of TV actress

Thelma Ritter. She was one of the first to call me to ask for information, and the next day came to my office to participate in a meeting with several newspaper reporters. She was totally supportive of the Corps and the recruit training and lamented the incident as one of those situations where everyone was trying to do the right thing. However, she had to agree with the thought I had already expressed that the Drill Sergeant made a couple of unfortunate decisions about training the recruits under such poor weather conditions.

As I neared the end of my second year at the Station, I was told by a friend in HQMC that I was going to be ordered to HQMC to become Head of the Recruiting Branch in the Department of Personnel. Shortly after I heard that, Brigadier General Robert O. Bare, Director of Personnel, came to New York to deliver a luncheon speech. I met him as he arrived by train and took him to the luncheon site. After lunch, I was taking him back to the train station and he said, "While I am here, I will tell you that you will be going to the U.S. European Headquarters in Paris, France for duty in July. How does that sound to you?"

My response was, "I could not be more overwhelmed. I had just heard a rumor that I would be going to Headquarters Marine Corps, and this is a big switch from that! Am I at liberty to share this news with my wife?"

He said, "You may share the news because the EUCOM Headquarters has officially accepted your assignment and there won't be any change. I'll send you a letter very soon with a lot more information."

I soon received word that I should get started on getting a passport. So, on a snowy Saturday morning, with Martha and the boys going to New York with me to get passport photos taken (they needed passports also), I was driving toward the George Washington Bridge on a heavy snow-covered road, straight on my side but a curve on the other side of the dual highway with a grass median strip area in between. A new Dodge car came around that curve at relatively high speed; the driver hit his brakes, which were frozen, so he jumped the grassy median strip and ran into our car head on. My almost-new Mercury was totaled, and so was the other car.

Brian, riding in the front seat beside me, was dressed in a heavily padded snowsuit. He was thrown against the windshield but was not hurt. Steve, in the back seat with Martha, was thrown against the back of the front seat and suffered a small cut but no significant injuries. Martha was thrown against the back of the front seat and had her teeth jarred but nothing broken. I suffered a crushed patella (kneecap) of the left knee and a large gash over my left eye. The first thing I remembered was being pulled out of the car through the passenger side because the car was lying on its left side. I was later told that I walked around to the front of the car, saw how badly it was damaged, and said, "My god. Look at my new car." Doctors told me later that, with that damaged left knee I was only able to walk around to see the front of the car because I was in total shock and didn't know what I was doing.

The next thing I remembered was being in an ambulance, headed for Englewood Hospital. A doctor there put a dozen stitches in the gash over my left eye and then told me that an ambulance would take me to the Naval Hospital out on Long Island. In that hospital, I remember lying on a stretcher in a hallway for a long period of time before a doctor arrived (it was a Saturday afternoon). The doctor who arrived was the surgeon who would operate on the knee, and he assured me that the operation would take place later that day. I remember asking him if the injury would prevent my staying in the Marine Corps. His answer was, "As a Lieutenant Colonel, the Marine Corps has a lot of money invested in you so we are going to do all we can to keep you fit for duty. If you were of lesser rank, we probably would give you a medical discharge."

I'm not sure his remarks were based on Marine Corps policy, but only reflected his personal opinion. He told me that he was not going to insert a material (metal, rubber or plastic) replacement knee cap because, in 15 to 20 years, it would give me a serious arthritic problem. In any event, the surgery was successful but I was in a hip-to-toe, full-length leg cast for six weeks and then had a period of very painful rehabilitation. The knee lasted until 1980, while I was in Japan, where I had some further surgery at the Naval Hospital, Yokosuka. Eventually, in 1992, in

Tallahassee, I had a total knee replacement which is still serving me very well.

When the time came to go aboard a U.S. transport ship and head for Europe, I was still using a cane but getting around very well. The ship was a great experience for Martha, Steve, and Brian, and after we arrived in Bremerhaven, Germany, I picked up my car (carried on the same ship) and we drove to Paris, arriving there on Bastille Day.

The United States European Command

(EUCOM)

My family and I traveled by troop ship from New York to Bremerhaven, Germany. After picking up our car, which was on the same ship, we drove to Paris, arriving there on 14 July, Bastille Day, a national holiday in France. Along the way we drove through small towns where people were dancing in the streets and otherwise celebrating their holiday, and it was a most colorful and interesting trip.

On arrival in Paris and checking in at EUCOM Headquarters, we were given temporary living spaces in Les Ibis Pension (the White Swans), an old French farmhouse and silo sitting on an island surrounded by a wide moat with a single-car bridge off a busy highway. It was a magnificent place to behold, with a dozen or more white swans swimming in the moat. Les Ibis was owned and operated by an attractive French woman who was an avowed Communist, but that did not interfere with her contracting her facility to the U.S. Government as temporary lodging for personnel reporting to EUCOM.

We were given two adjoining rooms up in the silo, a true adventure for us. Halfway up the steps to our rooms, the lights went out automatically and we were in total darkness. I had Martha and the boys stand still and I went up to the fourth landing platform where I fumbled around in the dark until I hit a light switch and the lights came on. Another adventure point.

The next morning, I reported to EUCOM Headquarters and was

escorted to the J-4 Section, Supply Branch, headed at that time by Colonel Lyman Stengel, Quartermaster Corps, U.S. Army. He welcomed me warmly and inquired about my family and whether we were doing all right at Les Ibis.

I assured him that we were all doing just fine but I said, "I am not sure what I can contribute to the supply branch since I have no experience as a supply officer. So might I ask what kind of job you have for me?"

"I have almost thirty years in the Quartermaster Corps of the Army," he responded. "In this Branch I have two Navy Supply Officers, two Air Force Procurement Officers, two civilians with contract experience, and an Army Officer from the Ordnance Corps. So I have all the supply, procurement, and contract experts I need. I need one Officer around here who has common sense and can supervise some administrative programs for reporting, and it will be your job to provide that common sense to keep us on the right path."

I said, "Thank you, Sir. I am relieved to know that I don't have to match the expertise you already have here. I will do my best to provide good common sense, and I am delighted to be here. Thank you for such a warm reception. Will I work directly for you or someone else?"

He said, "Your immediate boss will be LtCol Jack Richmond, U.S. Army, a fine officer and another one I can count on for good common sense." With that, he called his secretary on the intercom and asked her to send Colonel Richmond in. In just a minute, Jack Richmond came in, a very pleasant, good-humored officer for whom I developed a lot of respect for his professional expertise and his ability to get along with people.

In about two weeks, an apartment became available, and we moved to Beauregard Village, a U.S. Army housing area in the village of Saint Germain, just the other side of the SHAPE Headquarters. The Army provided us four cots, several blankets, and a few pieces of cookware. We found some empty orange crates, which we took home to use as tables. We lived that way for almost a month before our household effects arrived via Bremerhaven. We lived there with a mix of other Service families until we completed our tour at EUCOM.

The head of the J-4 Division was Major General McDonald, U.S. Air Force. When Colonel Stengel took me in to meet him, he put strong emphasis on one point. He said that my assignment to Europe presented a wonderful opportunity for me and my family to broaden our knowledge of the world, and that we must take every opportunity to travel and learn about the people of Europe and their cultures.

He showed me a chart on the wall that listed every J-4 Officer and displayed when they went on leave and which ones were not using their leave time. He said he expected that every officer would use all of the leave he had coming to him, that he checked that chart every week, and if I was not using my leave to take my family somewhere in Europe, he would call me in to explain to him why I was not doing so.

That was a brand new attitude about leave, but I understood his message and vowed to myself that I would do as he directed. Over my two years there, Martha and the boys and I put 15,000 miles on our Chevrolet traveling south to Italy, west into Germany, north to Sweden, and along the French coast to Normandy and other old European cities. It was a wonderful family experience for us, and a bonus on top of the job I had in the J-4 Division.

One of my jobs was to supervise the contracts of 24 Foreign Military Assistance Program (FMAP) projects. The FMAP was a joint program between the U.S. and several European countries in which the U.S. furnished the technical expertise and the host government provided the facility, the production machinery, and the labor to produce artillery shells, both casings and projectiles and other heavy ordnance items for storage in Europe. The products would be for host government consumption or for U.S. consumption if the U.S. had to fight in Europe again.

There were contracts in England, Scotland, Germany, Italy, and France, and the contracts were supervised by EUCOM Headquarters. My job was to summarize the reports which came in on the contracts quarterly and send the reports on to the Department of Defense. My job included visiting the production plants, kicking a few machines, and telling the contractors how well they were doing; or, in a couple of instances, urging them to catch up to the commitments on production.

The first inspection trip I made was a memorable one. The plant was just on the edge of Toulouse, France, a pleasant several hours train ride away. An Army Major from our Embassy in Paris was detailed to accompany me and serve as my interpreter. He was an American who had a French wife and was fluent in the French language. I was a Lieutenant Colonel, but he treated me like I was a General Officer. He purchased the train tickets, insured that my luggage was properly in hand, briefed me on the officials we would see, and was more an Aide than just an interpreter.

A letter was sent by EUCOM Headquarters to the Facility Manager advising him of my visit, and in the letter they said that I was "representing General Norstad," the NATO Commander in Paris. That was a stretch of the facts but it was not my doing. When we arrived at the railroad station in Toulouse, I stepped out of the railroad car on to a red carpet which had been laid out for my arrival. At the far end of the carpet (about 30 feet) stood a welcoming group of French folks to include a representative of the Mayor of Toulouse, the Manager of the plant I would inspect, and several other local dignitaries. My interpreter said that the red carpet was rolled out because I was "representing General Norstad."

There were four FMAP plants in France, each one managed by an expert in the field of ordnance, explosives, black powder, or brass shell casings. Each plant had an extensive dining facility, and in each of those facilities, there was an Executive Dining Room, used only by the plant director and several of the top people of the plant staff. The four directors knew each other very well, and they formed a Gourmet Dining Club. I was the honored guest at one of the gourmet evenings during my visit. During the briefing for me in the director's office, one of the executives said I should look out the window which overlooked a large field of asparagus plants. There, gardeners gathered fresh asparagus which I would enjoy later at dinner. It was a super dinner of five or six courses, each with a different, carefully selected French wine. The story does not end there.

These directors talked frequently with each other about business and gourmet food matters. The result was that, on my first visit to each plant in France, I was treated to a gourmet dinner with each director trying to out-do the previous one with an outstanding menu. These travels were a super bonus on top of all the other good things about the EUCOM tour of duty.

We lived in a walled American compound called Petite Beauregard, on the edge of Saint Germain. It was a nice, three-bedroom apartment with two baths and a small but adequate kitchen. For our first month, we slept on canvas cots, courtesy of the Army, utilized wooden orange crates from the Commissary as dining tables, and had a very Spartan lifestyle at home until our furniture arrived from Bremerhaven. We had very nice neighbors in our apartment building, three Air Force families and two Army families, and we all got along well together. We became very close with the family of Air Force Colonel Al Forsman, who lived across the hall from us on the first floor. He had six children and a nice wife who became a very close friend to Martha. Colonel Forsman was the Executive Officer of the Supply Branch, so we worked together a lot.

For part of our time there, we had two maids for the price of one. They were sisters from the Netherlands named Wimka and Seeska. They were very attractive blonde girls in their upper 20's, and their greatest reward from us was that Martha allowed both of them to take a soaking hot tub bath after the day's work. They had only a small shower with infrequent hot water where they lived in downtown Paris. They worked as a team, but we paid only for one worker. It must be remembered that, in 1956, Europe was still recovering from the war, jobs were hard to get, and the pay scale was low by current standards.

I developed a good relationship with then Brigadier General Donald Weller, USMC, who was the J-3 on the EUCOM staff. He was recognized as the premier expert in naval gunfire support at Iwo Jima and thereafter. We served together later at HQMC.

Nearing the end of my second year at EUCOM, I contacted my personnel monitor at HQMC and suggested that I get a new assignment. He told me the decision had already been made and that I would be coming back to Quantico to attend the Senior School at Quantico. The EUCOM assignment was most pleasant and professionally rewarding, but I was eager to get back to the Marine Corps.

The Senior School

The Senior School class was composed of lieutenant colonels and majors plus several equal rank officers from our allies like Korea and Canada. The School was located in Quantico, and many of us student officers were quartered in Thomason Park, a housing area on base out toward old Highway 1.

It was a comfortable year after the assignment in France, because the boys were back in American schools, the water was drinkable without boiling, and milk was ok no matter where you bought it. Martha could drive all over the area, and the boys had tons of friends. The Senior School had a reputation for being tough academically, and there were lots of early morning and late night exercises.

I knew a lot of the instructors personally, and that made it more enjoyable than it might have been had that not been the case. Having just come off of a joint service assignment, I had different views of some contentious joint issues than some of my fellow Marine Officers, who sometimes can only see joint issues through Marine Corps emblem eyeballs. There were several instances in which the School Director, Colonel Merrill Day, sought me out to compliment me on the comments I made during our seminars. I never was critical of our Marine Corps position on long-standing joint issues, but I had learned that every issue can look different, depending on where you view it from, and that there is more than one way to be right on a contentious issue. I should add here that Colonel Day wrote a very nice fitness report on me for the School term. The report made me realize that I had been more closely watched during Senior School than I knew.

Martha and I, through social programs in the class, made good friends with the Navy Officers in the class, and I became a good friend with an Officer from Brazil, all of whom enlarged my intellect about other Services and about our Allied Officers. All in all, Senior School was a pleasant and mind-expanding experience which I found most enjoyable.

A few weeks before graduation, a representative from HQMC Personnel Department came down and gave us information about out next duty stations. For me, it was not unexpected that I was going back to HQMC to the G-3 Section as a joint action officer. And that duty assignment, as I look back on it, was the most important to me professionally, because of the Marine Officers I worked for and the exposure it gave me to a number of General Officers who later sat as members of Selection Boards when I moved into promotion zones.

HQMC 1959-1962

Going back to HQMC was just the right move for me. After just finishing Senior School, and doing so with a modicum of success, and fresh off the joint service tour at EUCOM, I was totally prepared to take up duties as a Joint Action Officer. As luck would have it, I would serve under officers who knew me because I had worked with them or around them before. I also worked for some fine officers whom I had not known before, and that served to broaden my education and work experience. Not only that, but some of the other service officers I had worked with in EUCOM turned up on the service staffs in the Pentagon. I felt very much at home.

I was assigned to the G-3 Section of Plans and Policies, and my immediate boss was Colonel Regan Fuller, an intellectual, chain-smoking officer who was held in high esteem by Brigadier General Wallace M. Greene (who later became Commandant), who was the Chief of Staff. I had known General Greene since my 1946 tour at HQMC. The head of the G-3 Section was Colonel Bob Cushman (later Commandant). Colonel Cushman's executive officer was Colonel Russ Duncan, whom I had known before. And lastly, but firstly, there was the Commandant, General David Monroe Shoup, whom I knew well and he knew me.

Colonel Fuller and I were the "Joint Action Coordinators" in effect, in that all Joint Action papers which were routed to the G-3 for coordination were routed to us before going in to Colonel Cushman. That kept me in the know on virtually all Joint matters in HQMC.

Somehow, good fortune seemed to stay with me. Secretary of Defense Robert McNamara provided the JCS with a list of 62 questions to which he wanted their answers, and many of them would require extensive studies. One large question on the list had to do with whether it was a good idea to establish a "strike command," a force which would be ready to strike back immediately if we were attacked anywhere in the world.

We Marines believed that we were already prepared to perform the functions of such a "strike command," and we saw no need for a new organization. Furthermore, we knew that one of the Army objectives was to insure that the amphibious ships of the Navy were as available to the Army as to the Marine Corps. Another attempt to degrade the mission of the Marine Corps. The Army was kind of hung up on its own petard because, on one hand, some Army generals were suggesting that there wasn't much future for amphibious operations, but here they were fighting to put soldiers on amphibious ships.

From the very first time the Joint Staff produced a paper proposing the establishment of the strike command, I wrote a "purple paper" (a disagreement) with the need for a strike command. I soon learned that SecDef had already decided to establish a strike command, and that he just wanted a study to support his decision. I told that to General Shoup, and his response was that I might be right, but we would continue to oppose it anyway.

After a number of JCS sessions on the subject, the time had come to get a JCS decision and get the paper to Secretary McNamara. On the day when the agenda included the decision to establish the command, I was still writing "purples" opposing the idea. At the JCS meeting, the result was as expected. I had learned from my Army sources that SecDef had already chosen the first commander of the strike command, General "Tiger" Adams, U.S. Army.

When General Shoup returned to his office after the JCS meeting, he called me to his office, along with General Greene. He invited me to sit by his desk and started by saying, "You were right all along. SecDef did not ask a question; he wanted support for what he already planned to do. I want you to know that I tabled your purple and stated again my view that there was no need for such a command. There was no way for us to win, but perhaps this will show you that I sat there grinding my teeth as the decision became inevitable."

With that he handed me a new yellow number 2 pencil on which his teeth marks were clearly visible from the point up to the eraser. He then said, "You did good work, but there was no way we could win." I still have that pencil in my pile of artifacts, though it will not mean anything to anyone but me.

Only one other incident during that tour stands out in my memory bank and, once again, it is especially meaningful only to me. The Corps strength stood at 178,000, and it was the Commandant's view that we needed a strength of 192,000 to meet all of our commitments and to maintain our high degree of readiness. He wanted a quick staff study to prove the need for the additional forces, and directed General Cushman to conduct the study; I was assigned as the project officer.

After several weeks of intensive work and the participation by almost all the generals at HQMC and inputs for the Force Commanders at Atlantic and Pacific, it was time to prepare a briefing for the Commandant. I prepared the briefing and included a number of flip charts to highlight certain parts of the briefing. My first task was to brief Colonel Cushman, who gave it his ok. Next was to brief General Greene as the Chief of Staff. General Greene said it was a fine briefing, but I had to shorten it a lot before it would be ready for the Commandant. He then worked personally with me to tighten it up by eliminating useless words and using only the essential punch lines to support the conclusion and recommended action. It took several tries, but he thought we were ready to present to the Commandant.

With all the generals at HQMC present in the Commandant's office, I presented the briefing. When I concluded the briefing, General Shoup said, "Colonel, sit here by my desk," which I did. He then turned to General Greene and to the assembled generals and said, "I have just had one of the best briefings since I have been in this office. However, if you generals believe that the study will convince the SecDef and others that we need more Marines, you are very badly mistaken."

And with that he went on to tear down some of the assumptions of the study, berate some of the conclusions, and generally give all the generals a thorough tongue lashing, none of which needs to be documented here. When we were dismissed, General Shoup said to me, "You did your usual fine job. It is the generals who need to go back to the drawing board."

I said, "Thank you, Sir," and departed.

I learned that the action officers who worked on the JCS papers for their service bosses were very honorable and straightforward officers. We all somehow knew the value of being honest with each other, and there was never a case in which I was given false or misleading information about a service position on a JCS matter, no matter how we opposed a particular issue. It was in those days that the trend started toward the concept of jointness in all military matters, and today, successful joint tours of duty are a requirement for advancement. I fully accepted that concept then and believe in it now, but am still bitterly opposed to any concept of a single Chief of Staff for the Armed Forces, and want to insure that the SecDef cannot block the views of the Joint Chiefs of Staff from going to the President.

General Greene decided that HQMC needed a Command Center, a central point in the headquarters where he and the Commandant had instant communications with Marine commands worldwide and a point where commands around the world could be assured of direct contact with the those in the headquarters whom they needed to reach. Further, the Command Center would be tied in with JCS and other headquarters twenty-four hours a day. General Greene chose Colonel Regan Fuller to get that Command Center up and operating. What did that mean to me personally? It meant that I was the lone member of the joint operations section within G-3. That went on for a couple of months until Colonel Fuller was assigned to the Chief of Staff's office and he was replaced by Colonel Bob Owens, a very nice guy but not very current at that time about Joint service matters. I was lucky again. Bob Owens was a fine officer, was eager to learn, and was quite content at the outset for me to carry the whole load. One day he said that he would like to give the JCS briefing to the commandant on an agenda item and, of course, that was all right with me.

He prepared the briefing and the supporting flip charts himself and went into the briefing room with high confidence. After the briefing, the Commandant said he had a few questions and he peppered Colonel Owens with questions about the other service views.

Bob had not really discussed the agenda item in depth with the action officers of the other services. Bob was somewhat embarrassed about his lack of knowledge, but escaped with his skin intact, though it was clear that General Shoup was not totally happy.

When we returned to our office he said, "Don't you ever let me do that again. I have a new understanding about all the time you spend on the phone talking with the other services, but I am leaving the briefings to you from now on!" That incident did not damage his career in any way and was a great learning experience for him in dealing with General Shoup. Bob served as Chief of Staff of the MAF Headquarters in Danang part of the time I served in the G-3 Section of the MAF staff.

Moving on after a highly successful tour at HQMC, I was eager to get back with the troops, and once again I was fortunate. My orders were to report to the 1st Marine Division at Camp Pendleton, California, where I became Commander, 3rd Battalion, 7th Marine Regiment.

Commander, 3rd Battalion, 1st Marine Division and the Cuban Missile Crisis

I was delighted to get back to troop duty, and when I joined the 1st Marine Regiment, I was assigned as 3rd Battalion Commander. My Regimental Commander was Colonel Sidney Altman and my Division Commander was Major General Herman Nickerson. The battalion was in a "lock-on cycle in the transplacement plan," meaning, in general terms, that after the training at Camp Pendleton, we would stay intact and rotate overseas (to Okinawa) as a well trained, unified battalion with only enough replacements to fill any vacancies created during the training cycle.

I include now my remarks to the assembled battalion in our outdoor theater area, intending to give the troops information about my background and what they might expect from me as their new commander. I have copied these remarks from my handwritten notes that I used for my remarks. I used notes because I had very carefully crafted those remarks.

Our training was intense and followed a training schedule basically prepared at HQMC and FMFPAC to insure that all lock-on battalions followed the same training regime. I had a number of young Marines who needed special attention to keep them focused on their training. One incident involved a Marine Private First Class who just couldn't stay out of trouble. One weekend he walked out of the San Clemente Gate and went home to visit his girlfriend. He was three days on unauthorized absence, and on return, he was brought to my office for "office hours" where, as the Battalion Commander, I could inflict limited punishment for relatively minor matters. My policy was that, when a Marine came to me for office hours, he would be accompanied by his immediate superiors, fire team leader and squad leader, his platoon commander and his company commander.

As he stood before my desk, I asked him, "Why did you feel the need to go home without any authorization for liberty or leave?"

He responded, "I had to go see my girlfriend and I stayed longer than I meant to."

I asked, "What was so important about seeing your girlfriend?"

"She is pregnant," he replied.

I asked, "Well, you had already had your part in that situation. Why couldn't you wait to get permission before you left here?"

He said, "I did not think I would get approval, so I just left."

I said, "Marine, you seem to be having a hard time following the rules, and you are going to have to get better about that. I note that you have had several other problems along that line so I am going to give you some time all by yourself to think about how you are going to change and be a better Marine. I hereby award you five days on bread and water in the Division Brig. Do you have anything else to say?"

He said, "If you send me down to that brig, I am going to cut my wrists."

I said, "Ok, you may do that, but don't do it in my office and make a big mess. Sergeant Major, have this Marine escorted to the Division Brig and schedule him to return to this office when he is discharged from the Brig."

The Sergeant Major escorted him outside the building, whereupon the Marine pulled out a razor blade and cut (cut, not slashed) both wrists. The Sergeant Major and other Marines present put him on the ground, and while they applied a large bandage to each wrist, the

Sergeant Major came in to tell me what happened.

I said, "Tell that Marine my order still stands. I will see him again when he has served his sentence."

Why did I do that? First of all, as the Commander, I was not about to be intimidated by such a threat from a Marine under my command. Second, I knew that a lot of folks, not just Marines, who threaten to cut their wrists do a bad job of it and don't cut deep enough to get the artery (suggesting to me that they were not really serious but were looking for sympathy). Third, I reasoned that if he brought the razor blade with him even before he appeared for office hours, he planned to bluff me if he could, and I could not let that happen. The story did not end there.

After his release from the Brig, he came back to the company area and was brought immediately to my office. I asked him if he had spent some time thinking about how to be a better Marine.

He said, "I did, and I think I will be. But, Sir, I would like a transfer."

"Where would you like to go?" I asked.

He said, "Any where I can work in a motor pool, because I am a good mechanic."

"Ok, Marine," I responded. "I am going to take a chance on you. I will reassign you to the motor pool, and if you prove in thirty days that you have become a better Marine, I will make the assignment permanent. You are dismissed."

He did become a better Marine and eventually was promoted to Corporal.

President John Kennedy and Mr. Khrushchev of the Soviet Union were at loggerheads about the Russians putting cruise missiles in Cuba, thereby threatening the United States mainland. Cuba willingly accepted the missiles. President Kennedy finally told Mr. Khrushchev to take those missiles out or we would take them out for him. (The events leading up to the Cuban missile crisis took place over a period of time, but I see no need for me to review all that here).

My battalion had reached the point that we were ready for the Division Commander's inspection, which was very thorough, to include administrative records, equipment inspection, and a final review in battle gear in battalion formation. I had great confidence that we were ready for inspection in all matters, and I stood at the front of the battalion formation, eager to hear what General Nickerson had to say. As he approached me, I saluted and said, "Third Battalion 1st Marine Regiment ready for inspection, Sir."

He returned the salute and then said, "Congratulations, a very thorough inspection by my staff and by me make it very clear that this is the most combat-ready battalion in the 1st Marine Division. You may dismiss the troops at your discretion."

I said, "Thank you, Sir. These Marines have worked very hard to get to this point. I will inform them of your congratulations."

Shortly thereafter, the 1st Marine Division went on alert for movement to the Guantanamo Bay area of Cuba. The 2nd Battalion, under the command of LTCOL Bill Geftman, was the alert battalion at that time, so that battalion moved out via airlift for Cuba.

I was designated as the task force commander to take my battalion and a squadron of helicopters from the aircraft wing at El Toro and embark on the USS Iwo Jima. We were the first troop unit to embark on the recently commissioned Iwo Jima, berthed in San Diego. We would transit the Panama Canal (the first aircraft carrier to do so) and head for Guantanamo Bay. My mission was to land my battalion via helicopters at a major road junction north of Guantanamo Bay to preclude any Cuban reinforcements from getting to that area.

Major General Bill Fairbourn, USMC, the amphibious task force commander, told me at one of the briefings that I had the "white cross mission."

I asked him smilingly whether he meant "Navy cross mission," and he said, "No I meant white cross mission because the probability of your being overrun at that crossroads intersection is very high."

I did not pass that info on to my staff or to the troops!

As fate would have it, faced with overwhelming military force lying just offshore from Cuba, Mr. Khrushchev blinked and said he would dismantle and move the missiles out of Cuba. When I passed word to the troops over the ship's loudspeaker system, there were loud shouts of celebration. A number of those Marines, however, were disappointed that the operation was called off because they were so keyed up and so ready to fight they wanted to go into action. As a veteran of World War II and Korea, I didn't need any more combat at that time. Over the loudspeaker system, I also told them that, except for keeping their weapons clean and for daily exercise periods, I wanted them to enjoy the cruise back through the Panama Canal and up to San Diego. We all received an extra bonus when the fleet units were told to have two days liberty in Jamaica – a great place for liberty.

While in Jamaica, we all greatly enjoyed the tourist spots and, of course, the bars were overwhelmed by Marines and Sailors. I worried a little bit about whether there might be too much celebrating, resulting in troubling incidents. There was only one unhappy incident in my task force. Four marines who had too much to drink commandeered a horse and buggy, drove around at excess speed, and ended up with the horse and the wagon in a not very deep canal. Local officials did not charge them with any offense after they ponied up enough money to have the horse extracted from the canal, pay the estimated repair costs for the wagon and triple wages for the native cart driver. I felt blessed that so many troops had such a great time ashore with so little damage done.

Arriving back at Camp Pendleton, we spent a week in unpacking and refurbishing our equipment and holding discussions on lessons learned. I knew that my six-month cycle as a battalion commander was about to conclude and a new commander would come in to move the battalion to Okinawa in the transplacement cycle. So, as expected, Colonel Altman called me in to his office to tell me I was being transferred to the Division Headquarters for duty in the G-4 (Logistics)

Section.

The head of G-4 was Colonel Oscar Peatross, a soft-spoken Marine who had a great reputation as a leader, and I knew I had been lucky again. Oscar later distinguished himself in combat when he was one of the commanders in Operation Starlight, the initial amphibious landing in Vietnam. Later, he became a general officer whom I followed in a billet in HQMC.

There were several other fine officers in the G-4 Section, but my seniority as a Lieutenant Colonel put me in as the Section Executive Officer. One of the other officers was Hal Hatch, who really became a top-notch Logistics officer and finally retired many years later as a Lieutenant General in charge of the Installations and Logistics Department at HQMC.

When his tour ended, Colonel Peatross was transferred out of the section, and his relief was Colonel Walter Reynolds, a classmate from Senior School. While serving as the G-4 Executive Officer, I received my promotion to Colonel but was told I would remain in the G-4 section for a while longer. As it turned out, not for very much longer.

The Commanding General of the Fleet Marine Force, Pacific, in Honolulu was Lieutenant General Victor H. Krulak, referred to by the troops as "the Brute." He was "vertically challenged" but was a giant in every other way as a Marine General. He and a few members of his staff came to visit with the 1st Marine Division at Camp Pendleton, and General Nickerson hosted a reception in his honor. I had known and worked with General Krulak in Quantico and had ridden horses with him and competed against him in open jumping classes in Quantico horse shows. He seemed to remember all of that just as clearly as I did. When Martha and I went through the receiving line, he stepped back from the line and pulled Martha with him. He had a few words with her which I could not hear. When we finished the receiving line, I said to her, "All right, what did General Krulak say to you so privately?"

She said, "He told me that he would be seeing us in Honolulu, because he had an assignment for you on his staff. He didn't tell you that?"

I said, "No, he did not. But I will try to find out more about it."

Later in the evening, when I talked with General Nickerson, I said to him, "Sir, I have heard a rumor here tonight that I am about to be transferred. May I ask if you are aware of that rumor?"

"Yes, the rumor is true," he responded. "You are going to be the Deputy G-4 on the FMFPAC staff, and you should be flattered that General Krulak has arranged with HQMC for your transfer. He is a tough guy to work for, but you will be a better Marine if you survive the experience."

And so it came to pass, I was transferred to FMFPAC Headquarters and became the Deputy G-4, another great assignment where I worked for and with a staff of fine Marine officers, most of whom had been handpicked by General Krulak.

Headquarters, Fleet Marine Force,

Pacific: Pathway to Vietnam

Because of Martha's fear of flying, I applied for transportation by ship to Hawaii, and the result was far beyond my expectations. Martha, Brian, and I were transported via the Lurline, a commercial cruise ship which operated between Los Angeles and Honolulu; in those days, a first-class operation by any standard. It was even suggested to me that I have my evening dress uniform available for the Captain's final evening reception. Our accommodations were first-class in every way.

When we arrived in Honolulu, we were met at dockside by General and Mrs. Krulak and delivered us to our temporary quarters in the Makalapa guesthouse. Mrs. Krulak (Amy) took Martha and Brian in one car and General Krulak and I were in a separate car. We were treated like old friends and family. As General Krulak departed from the guesthouse he said, "I'll see you in the morning."

The next morning, I was in my new office at 0730. At 0750, Colonel Feeley's phone rang, and one of the Marines in the office answered, it simply saying, "Colonel Feeley's office." After a brief pause, he said, "Yes, Sir." He turned to me and said, "General Krulak wants principal staff members in his office at 0900."

I asked those in the immediate vicinity, "When does Colonel Feeley usually get here?"

The answer was, usually by eight o'clock, but he must have a problem this morning.

I said, "I will go to General Krulak's office. Let Colonel Feeley know that I am there."

Arriving at General Krulak's office, I noted a sign on his door which read, "You may express any opinion you wish in this office. Just be sure your facts are correct."

I went and sat in an open seat, with no chance to even say hello to the other staff principals who were there. General Krulak was writing on some papers at his desk and did not seem to even notice that we were assembled. After a minute or so, he dropped his pen, pushed the papers aside, and looked to see who was present in his office. When he looked at me there was no smile, no semblance of recognition, and he asked, "Are you the G-4?"

I responded, "Yes, Sir, at this moment I am."

He then went on talking to those assembled about his concerns at that time. I kept asking myself, is this the same general who received me so warmly yesterday? It was just his way of doing business, and I do not fault him for that. That incident reinforced what I already knew: There are times to be friendly with your boss and at all other times to be strictly professional. I decided then and there that, when working with General Krulak, I would let him set the tone of the moment.

Colonel Jim Feeley was a naval aviator, a fine Marine officer who sometimes had a short-fuse temper, and when he was upset, his face and his mostly bald head became fiery red. We got along very well together, and I thought we functioned well together as the G-4 and the Deputy G-4. In the G-4 Section at that time, there were three Marines with whom I developed friendships which lasted a long time. They were Lieutenant Colonel Ike Fenton, who had been a close neighbor in Quantico back in the early 1950s; Lieutenant Colonel John Miller, who later became a Lieutenant General and died not long after his retirement; and Sergeant Karen Pond, a clerk typist, who was a very efficient clerk but also a very attractive woman Marine who later became a Second Lieutenant and eventually retired as a Captain.

When Sergeant Pond's enlistment was about to expire, I called her in for an interview about her plans for reenlisting or for accepting a discharge. Her family had some difficult problems at that time, and I suggested that she might be better off if she reenlisted. I told her that she should work on her shorthand and other secretarial skills, and I said, very straightforwardly, "Karen, if you will develop your secretarial skills, you have the looks, the personality, and the social skills that every commander would like to have outside his office, and I suggest that you work toward that goal."

She did just that. I lost track of her for a couple of years. Then I learned that she was the secretary to Brigadier General Jay Hubbard (naval aviator) who recommended her for officer training. At her graduation and commissioning as a Second Lieutenant, General Hubbard and I pinned on her new Second Lieutenant bars. She went on to become a Captain and married a Lieutenant Colonel (too much her senior with two almost grown daughters). Eventually, the marriage did not work out. She retired as a Captain and went to work for a defense contractor (Boeing, as I recall). Some time after she left Boeing, she hit a slot machine jackpot for $50,000 and wisely bought a small house.

In 1963, we had a Marine helicopter squadron in Vietnam providing air support and transportation to South Vietnamese Marines, mostly down in the Delta area. General Krulak appointed me a the primary point for contact for that squadron, with instructions to me to be sure that squadron was always adequately supplied. About every three months, I went to Vietnam to personally visit the squadron commander, Colonel Keith McCutcheon, and check on the squadron's logistic status.

I had come to know Keith McCutcheon when I was in the development center and he was in command of HMX-1, the presidential helicopter squadron. When I visited with him, he always had me stay in his tent quarters and insured that I had transportation to get around as necessary during my visits. He was a superb Marine, a top-notch aviator, and was promoted to four-star rank on his deathbed in Bethesda Naval

Hospital. He died while serving as Assistant Commandant.

It was during my FMFPAC HQS tour that I first knew and worked with then Colonel Bob Barrow (later Commandant) when he was the Deputy G-3 while I was the Deputy G-4. We both made several trips to Vietnam with General Krulak and joined together to write the after-trip reports. On the way back to Honolulu from one of those trips to Vietnam, I was sitting alone with General Krulak in his compartment on the airplane and we were reviewing our visits with the troop units. I said, "There is one part of our system that we have to do something about, and I am still pondering how to do it. Currently our battalions send their supply requisitions to Regiment where they are consolidated and sent on to Division where they are consolidated and sent directly to the supply depot in Philadelphia, Pennsylvania. That consolidation process is time consuming with unnecessary duplication. When the supply depot ships the equipment to Vietnam, the procedure is reversed. When Division breaks down the shipment for the regiments, the regiments have to break it out for the battalions. The current process wastes time and effort and simply means that at the company and battalion level, where resupply is most critical, they wait an inordinate amount of time for a spare part or replacement item that is needed down at the combat level. I will discuss this with our supply officer when we get back to Honolulu and give you a recommendation for change. It would be so much simpler if we could get the depot to package their shipments for each battalion, give it a special identification by a big red ball or some other readily identifiable logo, and ship it straight to the battalions."

General Krulak responded, "I've got the picture. You are absolutely right. When I am back in my office, I will call the depot directly and tell them that is what I want the depot to do. We don't need the commandant's involvement or risk any objection. What should we call the program?"

After talking about it further, he decided to call it the Red Ball Express Program, and the next morning in his office, he set that up by direct phone call to the depot. He then directed our supply officer, Colonel Chan Olsen (later Major General and head of the supply department at HQMC), to write up the instructions for the program and then called the Commandant to let him know that the Red Ball Express Program would be underway within two weeks. A man of action! He gave me credit for the idea in my next fitness report.

The good point about my trips to Vietnam was that I learned a lot about that country and the people well before I went there for duty; very useful.

There is one other incident that is a special memory. General Krulak appeared to get along just fine with General Westmoreland, U.S. Army, Commander of the U.S. Forces in Vietnam, but there was one other officer, Lieutenant General William E. DePuy, U.S.A., the J-3 of the MACV staff, with whom he frequently crossed swords (literally). General Krulak and General DePuy were very much alike physically (vertically challenged), and both were very decisive officers who made no efforts to conceal their views. General Krulak wanted to deploy a hawk battalion (anti-aircraft missiles – our first one) in the vicinity of the Chu Lai Airfield, base of the 1st Marine Airwing. General DePuy was very much opposed to that deployment and argued strongly against it. General Krulak decided to take the bull by the horns and got the Commandant to agree to the deployment.

One day General Krulak called me to his office and said, "I'm sending you on a special mission to Saigon. You are going to deliver a special, personal message to General DePuy. I will arrange for him to receive you when you arrive, and here is the message: "I am going to deploy a hawk battalion to the I Corps area in the vicinity of the Chu Lai Airfield. I wanted to send a special messenger to give you this information because I know you are opposed to it, but my decision is final. Further details will follow."

The next morning, I was on an Air Force plane headed to Saigon. Air Force protocol is very efficient, and as a Colonel on courier business, I had a prime seat and special attention during the flight. A Marine officer met me at the Saigon Airport and drove me straight to MACV headquarters. Within minutes, I was in General DePuy's office. He asked me to have a seat while he was on the phone. With that completed, he turned to me and very cordially asked about my flight and how things were in Honolulu. With the pleasantries out of the way, he said, "I understand you have a message to me from General Krulak."

I said, "Yes, I do. General Krulak said that I should inform you that he is going to deploy a hawk battalion to the I Corps area in the general vicinity of the Chu Lai Airfield. He sent me here with that personal message because you are opposed to the deployment, but his decision is final and he will provide additional information later."

He said, "Is that the entire message?"

I said, "Yes, Sir, that is the entire message."

"I will deal directly by phone with General Krulak on this matter," General DePuy said. "Thank you for your efforts in delivering the message."

I said, "Thank you, Sir," and departed his office.

Outside his office, a Marine officer was waiting for me. He said that the J-4 wanted to see me. The J-4 was Major General Evans, U.S. Army, whom I had met at Camp Lee, Virginia, when my brother-in-law, Bob Allen (USNR Retired and PhD, UVA) worked for him in a civilian capacity. General Evans said he saw my name on the protocol list and wanted to invite me to dinner that night at the Grand Hotel in Saigon. I couldn't resist that offer and learned that Saigon provided first-class food and surroundings for those who could afford it. A most memorable evening.

I was involved in a real fun event called the "Pearl Harbor Mardi Gras," an entertainment event sponsored by the Navy Officers' Wives Club at Pearl Harbor. The club advertised widely, seeking folks to audition as singers or dancers, or to otherwise help with set building, lighting, and other support functions for a first-class musical evening. I was singing in the Camp Smith Chapel Choir and had sung several times at the Officer's Club at Camp Smith, so several folks insisted that I audition for the Mardi Gras. When I auditioned, I sang, "On the Street

Where You Live" from "My Fair Lady." They stopped me when I was halfway through and said, "No need to do it all. You are in and you will sing that song in a prominent place in the program."

The event was performed for three nights at the Officer's Club in Pearl Harbor and was sold out all three nights. The first night was called Navy Night, the second was Marine Corps Night, and the third was Joint Service Night. The program was advertised at Pacific Air Force Headquarters and Fort Shafter. For the Friday night performance, the entire officer corps of FMFPAC Headquarters and a few from Marine Corps Air Station, Kaneohe, were in attendance.

In addition to my solo number, I joined three Navy officers to form a barbershop quartet, and we were a bigger hit than any other act in the show. I sang tenor, of course, and we always concluded our three-song set with, "Will someone please speak kindly to the tenor?" In those days, I could hit the B-flat just a half-step below two octaves above Middle C. I had the last five notes to myself, and after I hit that top note and held on to it, the other three spelled out t-e-n-o-r and we held it for twelve beats. It brought the house down all three nights. The three Navy officers who performed with me became good friends.

There were some really top-notch singers and dancers in the cast, and we had a professional director who knew how to get the best out of his cast members. The show was a big hit on each night and we all regretted that it had to end. Somewhere in my artifacts, I have an audio cassette tape of the show. It was a most memorable event, and I made lots of new friends in the Navy and in Honolulu, some of whom I saw in later years, either in Honolulu or in Washington, DC.

We lived in a town house in the Makalapa housing area and had a most comfortable set up. We had Navy neighbors who became good friends, and Brian did well in Punahou School. Martha spent a lot of time working in the Naval hospital and working with the Red Cross, mostly assisting families who were leaving Honolulu as their husbands went on to Vietnam or serving cookies and snacks to the stream of servicemen headed back home after service in Vietnam. I was one of those who were headed next to Vietnam. Martha and the boys took the Lurline again to Los Angeles. I took air transportation so I could get there ahead of them to pick up the car (which went by separate ship) and arrange for accommodations before we started to drive across country. That trip was uneventful but good for all of us. After I had a few days leave, I flew back to Honolulu, stayed in a motel by the airport, and went on to Vietnam.

My Vietnam Tour and the Industrial College of the Armed Forces

I had no advance information before arriving in Vietnam about what my assignment would be. I was enormously pleased when I was assigned as Commanding Officer, 7th Marine Regiment, 1st Marine Division, operating at that time just north of the city of Chu Lai, relatively close to the Marine Air Base, and that I would be working with the 1st Vietnamese Army Division and the Korean Marine Brigade. I established good relationships with commanders of those units, and we performed a number of Joint military operations in the I Corps area and enjoyed success in every one of our operations.

I relieved Colonel Bill Crossfield, who had commanded the regiment for six months, the standard tour length for regimental commanders. I was fortunate to inherit some very capable staff officers, including Major Ed Fitzgerald (Regimental S-3), Major Gerry Turley (Regimental S-4), and Captain Dick Alger in the S-2 section. I was greatly pleased by an experienced, no-nonsense kind of senior NCO as my Regimental Sergeant Major. He and I shared our pyramidal tent hootch. As the Regimental Sergeant Major, he had a fine relationship with other senior NCOs in the division and in the MAF Headquarters, located in Danang.

I choose not to describe combat experiences because these many years later my memory for accurate details is somewhat lacking. The war aspects of Vietnam are well documented in hundreds of books and magazines and I don't believe I can add anything useful to that history.

General Nickerson visited me often and frequently visited my front-line units without letting me know until the visit was over. On one occasion, he relieved one of my battalion commanders and did not tell me until he was back in his division headquarters. I later told him that I was disappointed in not being involved in that decision, but he said he did what was best for the regiment at that time. There was nothing else I could do about that situation.

On several occasions, I took operational control of one or two battalions of the 5th Marine Regiment for extended area sweeps against Viet Cong units. I never faced a large Viet Cong organized unit, but was forever chasing small units which concentrated their efforts against village chiefs to persuade them not to cooperate with us. The problem was that some village chiefs acted as if they were strongly with us, but at nighttime, they cooperated and operated with Viet Cong units. We were in the area of the "dirty war," where we faced booby traps, bamboo-spiked pits, and locally rigged explosive devices (now called IEDs - Improvised Explosive Devices). Many of my Marine casualties lost arms, legs, or both as we swept through grassy areas, rice paddies, and light jungle growth. We did not face the heavy jungle growth faced by Marine units in other areas of Vietnam.

The pacification program was underway at that time, and I was often directed to place a squad of Marines in a small village to provide security at night. On a number of occasions, those squads were overrun by Viet Cong night attacks, which often had cooperation from within the village. As part of the pacification program, we provided protection for villages during rice harvest so all the villagers could work at harvesting and the rice could be denied to Viet Cong forces.

It was most interesting to work with the 1st Vietnamese Army and the Korean Marine Brigade commanders. I visited a number of village chiefs with them and had to have some food and drink with them. The food was not at all to my liking, but I ate and drank in the interest of establishing good relations at the village level. The Vietnamese Army Division had a military assistance group of us Army advisors which operated at the division level. Colonel Ochs, U.S. Army, a member of a prominent New York City family, was the senior advisor and one of the finest army officers I ever knew. It was a pleasure to work him and the other members of his group. He had a couple of helicopters that stayed with him at the division command post, and he dispatched them often to pick me up at my command post and take me down to his location to confer with his boss, the Army Division Commander.

The Army helicopter pilots mostly were warrant officers and they were masters of their trade. On several occasions, Marine helicopters were standing down because of poor weather and were not available to me. Colonel Ochs said weather didn't bother his pilots, so they provided my transportation, flying at extremely low altitudes but always accomplished their mission. Other than those times of marginal weather conditions, helicopter support provided to me by the First Air Wing was superb. On more than one occasion, we received small arms fire as we descended or departed landing areas as I visited my front-line units. Luckily, no one in the helicopter was ever hit by the bullets which penetrated the skin and entered the cabin of the helicopter.

The Korean Marine Brigade was a tough bunch of fighters who tried in every way to emulate their U.S. Marine Corps brothers. They were highly disciplined. In one instance, a Korean Marine raped a Vietnamese girl. Before the brigade troops standing in formation at their compound, the offender was marched out in front of the Brigade Commander, who used his pistol to shoot the offender in the head. The troops watched as the deceased was carried off the field. I did not hear of another rape case in that brigade during my time in Vietnam.

The Vietnamese Army Commander invited me and the Korean Brigade Commander to dinner at his home in Chu Lai City. It was a mansion by local standards, with a mix of local and U.S. style furniture and a beautiful outside patio complete with a koi pond. After dinner, we went out on the patio to have brandy and cigars. Our dinner included sparrow heads (complete with their beaks) and fine steaks (courtesy of Colonel Ochs).

During the conversation, the division commander asked us how we enjoyed the dinner. I said mine was delicious and could not have been better. The Korean General said it was a great dinner, but he missed having garlic. With that, the Army Commander directed an aide who hustled into the house and quickly returned with a silver platter full of raw garlic. I declined, saying that I was too full of dinner and so did Colonel Ochs, but the other two ate the garlic like peanuts. The odor was most unpleasant to me, but I had no way to escape. One of the Army helicopters took me back to my CP close to midnight. A night of mixed emotions, but on balance very favorable in building trust and confidence between the three of us as commanders.

While I was commanding the 7th Regiment, Lieutenant General Ray Davis, Medal of Honor recipient, was serving as Director of the Personnel Department at HQMC. During his visit to the 1st Division, he stopped in my command post to have lunch and a briefing about my regimental operations. I met him when he arrived by helicopter, shared lunch with him and the regimental staff, gave him a briefing about our operations, and then escorted him to the helicopter pad.

As we said goodbye, he said, "I want you to know that, back at headquarters, you are viewed as highly competitive in the zone for Brigadier General. You have had several high-pressure jobs and did well in all of them. You are doing a fine job out here. Of course, I cannot guarantee anything, but I think you have grounds for being optimistic."

I thanked him for sharing that with me and said I had not been giving that lot of thought lately, but I was encouraged by what he said.

He said, "Thanks for lunch. I'll see you in Washington." I did not share that conversation with anyone, but it was a conversation I would not forget.

As expected, in the middle of my sixth month as Regimental Commander, I received word that I would be moving to the MAF staff and joining the G-3 Section. Lieutenant General Lou Walt was commanding the MAF at that time, and I looked forward to working with him. The head of the G-3 Section was Colonel Jim Barrett, with whom I had worked very closely in HQMC. Also joining the G-3 Section was Colonel Fred Haynes, who had just commanded the 5th Marine Regiment. So, in a way, it was kind of old-home week. We all got along together with no disagreements to speak of, so it was pleasant duty. All we did was work, go to lunch, work, go to dinner, work, catch a few hours of sack rest, and then work some more. We didn't stand regular watch hours; we worked according to what needed to be done and took short breaks when we could.

General Walt was dedicated to being out with the troops every day. Jim Barrett, Fred Haynes, and I rotated on accompanying General Walt on those visits. General Walt, known to the troops as the "big, blue eyed squad leader," would gather a small group of Marines, have them sit down and relax, and after telling them what a fine job they were doing, solicit questions. He usually got some very pointed questions. Those were the Marines he wanted to visit and talk to every day. He was most effective talking to troops down at that level.

General Walt was relieved by Lieutenant General Bob Cushman, who brought in Brigadier General Bob Owens as his Chief of Staff. I had worked closely with both of them back in HQMC, so once again I was working for and with seniors who knew me and whom I knew, so it continued to be a comfortable relationship for me.

As I was heading home after my Vietnam tour, my son Steve was literally passing me in mid-air en route to Vietnam to start his tour. Martha simply transferred her worrying about me to worrying about Steve. Good fortune prevailed; we both had successful tours, and neither of us suffered any wounds of war. As an artillery forward observer, Steve's duties were much more dangerous than mine were.

My orders from HQMC directed me to report to the Industrial College of the Armed Forces (ICAF), located at Fort McNair, Washington, DC, for "duty under instruction" (student). I had hoped that I would attend the National War College, but my extensive background in logistics made the Industrial College a more logical assignment. In hindsight, I think it worked out as the best solution. The contacts I made there served me well in my later assignments and as we were increasingly stressing "jointness," I know that having good friends and contacts in the other services was of great importance.

And so, on to Fort McNair and the purchase of a house on Wayburn Drive in Annandale. Before I left Vietnam, I bought a new Volkswagen Bug through an American car dealer who operated through the Army/Air Force Exchange System (AAFES). I paid only $1250 for it but had to pick it up from the ship at dockside in Baltimore. It was a great car which served me particularly well as I drove around the beltway from Annandale to Fort McNair. One of the best financial deals I ever made.

I was the first member of my ICAF class to reach the rank of Brigadier General, though several others in each service made that big step shortly thereafter. All things considered, it was a good year. I finished in the top 25% of the class and the Commandant of ICAF wrote a special letter to the Commandant of the Marine Corps commending me on my good work. For my special project, I wrote about the declining railroad industry, saying that the railroads believed they were in the railroad business and wrongly so. They were in the transportation business. Later, grudgingly, they began to haul the trailers of the eight eighteen-wheeler trucks, and it slowly rejuvenated the railroad industry. Previously, they had viewed the trucking industry as rivals and would not haul those trailers. Today you can see trains of twelve or more flat cars loaded with those big trailers, minus the prime movers, and both industries are better off because of it. My main point of the paper was to stress the important role of trains in our national security. I continue to be concerned about the declining welfare of our railroad industry as related to its importance to our national security.

And so, back once again to duty at HQMC, the big selection board and Harvard University.

The Big Selection Board and the Advanced Management Program, Graduate School of Business, Harvard University

Back again at HQMC, I awaited the results of the Brigadier General selection board. Like always, I had a plan if I was not selected. My reasoning was that, if I missed selection the first time before a board, my chances of being picked by the next board would be very slim, so I should retire and get started on a second career. At the back of my mind was the offer from Colonel Jim Tinsley in Cleveland to go to work for him if I did not get selected. I had been encouraged by General Ray Davis' remark that I was considered "very competitive" by a number of the generals in HQMC, so I was really caught in the middle as I awaited the results of the board.

When the board finished its work, I received a call from Major General Jim Masters, who simply said, "You will like the results of the board." And of course, when the list was made public a couple of days later, I did. The questions then turned to when will I be promoted and where might I go for duty.

My promotion took place in the office of the Commandant, General Leonard Chapman, attended by my mother, Martha, Brian, the generals in the headquarters, and a few civilian friends of long standing. After the swearing in and presentation of my personal flag, those present lined up to congratulate me and speak to my family. At the end of the line was Lieutenant General William K. Jones, director of Personnel. As he shook hands with me, he said, "I'll see you in the morning at 0900 in your new office next to mine."

Since HQMC did not function on Saturday morning, I said, "Tomorrow morning?"

He said, "Yes, tomorrow morning, nine o'clock sharp."

I said, "Yes, Sir. I'll be there."

I was in my new office at 0745. The secretaries had prepared my office to include the national colors and my personal flag behind the desk and an array of pens, pencils, and note pads on the desk. Promptly at 0900, General Jones walked in. He said, "Good morning. Welcome to the world of Marine Corps general officers, a world to which many aspire but only a few attain. Let's talk about what your duties are."

He made it clear that I was there to carry out the policies of the Commandant, but that I had the authority to make exceptions to those policies when circumstances suggested otherwise. When I made exceptions to current policy, I must inform him so he would be prepared to respond to the Commandant if he needed to. He stressed the importance of coordination with the rest of the HQMC staff, saying that we must insure that we all work for the same Commandant and we must not let any decision get caught up in improper staff work. He was a great Marine officer to work for, and I learned so much that served me well in my years as a general officer.

One afternoon when General Jones was out of the office, the Chief of Staff, Lieutenant General William J. Van Ryzin, called me in to say that I would be attending a special advanced management course at Harvard University in Boston. "You will not be taking your family up there, but you have time to get them settled before you go. When you get back from that course, I have in mind a different job for you, but we will talk about that later."

And so, off to Boston I went. I drove so I would have wheels available to me if I needed them, and that was good decision.

The advanced management program (AMP) was designed as a "mind stretching" course for corporate executives who were already stars in their own corporations but who were being groomed for even higher-level corporate executive positions. We were organized into "can groups" for room assignments and for study groups. Each group had a manufacturing specialist, a financial expert, a marketing specialist, and a labor specialist, and I was designated as the stockholders and government representative.

My roommate and manufacturing rep was from Timken Bearing Co. in Cleveland; our finance guy was the treasurer of Nabisco, our international guys (we had two) were from Australia and Brazil; our small business rep was from Baltimore; our marketing guy was from Northern Telecom; and our sales rep was from Brunswick. It was a highly professional group, and all did well in subsequent years in their respective corporations.

The can group housed two men to a bedroom (two single beds, a small chest of drawers, and a slender closet), with four bedrooms opening into a social room and a bathroom designed for eight people. The accommodations were Spartan and well below what those corporate executives were used to, but for an old grunt Marine, the accommodations were just fine. The can groups consisted of representatives from corporate finance, manufacturing, engineering, marketing, sales, a senior foreign manager, government representative, and a small business owner. We worked as a team on business cases (based on real corporate situations), and the professors really poured on the requirements for after-class work. It was a very full schedule of class and homework for the entire ten weeks, and I felt it truly was a mind-broadening experience.

Two events happened early in the course which established me as "the General" with the entire class. On the second day, we went on a bus tour of Boston. On my bus there was my roommate, who was seated near the rear of the bus, and I was seated near the middle. Waiting for the departure time, there were comments about the delay. My roommate spoke up so that he was heard throughout the bus, "I'll bet the Marines could get all this straightened out."

I said, "John, if you keep saying nice things about Marines, I'll let you call me by my first name."

An unidentified voice yelled out, "What's that?" to which I responded, "General."

That brought a roar of laughter from the loaded bus. Those remarks were repeated to all those on the other bus, and I received my first identity marker.

The other event occurred in the middle of the first week. We were receiving a lecture and seminar discussion on labor/management relationships, and our nationally known labor expert was stressing the importance of keeping the workforce happy. He was facing the left side of the classroom when he suddenly turned around to the right side, where I was seated, and said, "General, when you get all those young Marines in intensive training, they are tired and want to quit. How do you keep them happy?"

In an instant, I replied, "We tell them they are happy and they are!"

Even the professor joined in the applause and the laughter. That was my second and most significant identity marker as a Marine and as a General.

The can group went to downtown Boston a couple of times a week to enjoy fresh seafood at some of the nation's finest restaurants. With their unlimited credit cards, they didn't care about the high costs of those pricey (but outstanding) eating places. We government reps explained to our several can groups that we were not able to do that, but every group had the same attitude. The other members in the groups uniformly said that they would take care of the dining costs and we government types could find some other way to contribute. In my case, there was a simple solution.

As an active duty Marine, I had access to the Class VI (wine, beer, spirits) store on the Air Force base on the suburbs of Boston and, in my favor, that Class VI facility was managed by a retired Marine Corps Gunnery Sergeant who I had known at HQMC. On my first trip there, he said, "General, you can buy anything you want here. You will not be limited in quantity, and I will be sure you get the sale prices when we have them."

So, my contribution to the can group was to be the purchasing agent for their Class VI supplies, and that made them very happy that I could buy at such favorable prices. Though each of them were personally well off financially, they took great pleasure in getting their wine and spirits at discounted prices. Maybe that is why they were financially so successful!

The final week of class most members brought their wives in to share in the social events, but Martha did not want to make the trip to Boston by herself and did not want to leave the boys, so I was solo for the events that week. The day after the course was completed, I wanted to get an early start on driving home. So, at 6 a.m., I departed the parking lot and at the very moment I hit the street in Boston, the first snowflakes of the season hit my windshield. I was out of the Boston area before the snow amounted to anything, and happily so. It was a great experience, but I was glad to have it behind me and was eager to find out what my new job would be at HQMC.

The Final Four

The final four years of my 37-plus years of active duty were spent at Headquarters Marine Corps in two of the most enjoyable jobs in my career. First, I was the JCS Operations Deputy (OPDEP), and my final two years, I was Chief of Staff, HQMC. I was more than just qualified for both of these jobs.

In the spring of 1975, I was completing my third year as Chief of Staff, U.S. Forces, Japan when I received a call from LtGen. Lou Wilson (he was Commanding General, Fleet Marine Forces, Pacific, headquartered in Honolulu). He had just returned from Washington, DC, and had been told that he would become the Commandant on 1 July. He said, "I want you to come back and be my JCS Operations Deputy, and of course, you will be a Lieutenant General. Can you get there by 1 July?"

I congratulated him and then told him it would take his intervention with CINCPAC, Admiral Noel Gayler, and with Ambassador Mansfield, because they were responsible for my staying in Japan for my third year. I told him that I would call each of them and tell them that General Wilson was giving me the opportunity to get my third star, and I hoped they would go along with that.

I did, and they did! However, the best I was able to do was to get back to HQMC on 1 August. I took over the OPDEP position on 1 September.

Because of my previous joint assignments in EUCOM and U.S.S Forces Japan, I had numerous contacts in each of the other Services and throughout the JCS Staff. I was, therefore, completely comfortable in my new assignment. One of the plusses about the job was the opportunity to get to know the heads of the other Services and their senior generals, senior officials in the Defense Department, and some senior officials of the State Department. Socially, it provided the chance to rub elbows with a lot of senior government officials that I otherwise would not have known. It also provided the opportunity to join in several social events in the White House with President Jimmy Carter.

Martha and I lived in Quarters 4 at the Marine Barracks, 8th and I Streets, SE, and that was an enjoyable experience. Our front yard was the Parade Ground, so we saw a lot of parade rehearsals, Evening Parades, and performances by the "President's Own" Marine Corps Band and the Drum and Bugle Corps. Martha was the chief cheerleader for the Drum and Bugle Corps, and they knew it. On the day of my retirement, after I had departed for the office, the Corps formed in front of our Quarters and performed a short concert to thank her for her support. They presented her with a drumhead which every member of the group had signed. There was a bonus for a while, in that son Stephen was stationed at the Barracks and served as a VIP Escort for the Evening Parades. Several times, he escorted his mother to her up-front seat!

General Wilson's only charge to me as the OPDEP was, "Don't ever let me be surprised at a JCS meeting." Other than that, he let me run the joint side of our Marine Corps business.

As we neared the end of two years in that job, General Wilson told me that I would move to the position of Chief of Staff, HQMC, and provided a job that I thought I was well prepared for – and I was. My first response to him was that I had two years as a Lieutenant General, and perhaps I should retire and provide room for a new Lieutenant General. He responded by saying that he would not permit me to retire, because I was a strong competitor to be his successor as Commandant. I really had not thought much about that possibility, but it was quite comforting to hear him say that.

My final words were, "I hope you are never sorry that I was your Chief of Staff."

He responded by saying, "That's the last thing I have to worry about."

We never talked about that again.

I did not do a lot to change the way the Chief of Staff office worked, but I did make a greater effort to reach out to our Senior Civilian executives to make them feel a more important part of the Marine Corps Team, and I know they appreciated my efforts. General Wilson let me run the Headquarters in my own style, and I appreciated his confidence and his allowing me to do it my way.

In my first meeting with all the General Officers assigned to HQMC, I told them I expected them to take full responsibilities for their billets, to act like the generals that they were, to carry out the Commandant's policies, to make exemptions from policy when supported by strong evidence, but never, never let me or the Commandant be surprised. I made it clear that I was not the decision maker; that was the role of the Commandant. Said another way, if I did not concur with some particular action or their proposed policy change, we would go together to present our views to the Commandant and let him make the decision.

I may be biased, of course, but I think HQMC worked very smoothly under my direction as Chief of Staff. When I retired, General Bob Barrow, named as the next Commandant, planned to combine the offices of Chief of Staff and Assistant Commandant. I told him very straightforwardly that I viewed that as a serious mistake; that, in my view, the Assistant Commandant had enough to do filling in for the Commandant, that the General Officers on the staff deserved a Chief of Staff who was devoted full-time to them and their problems. He did it his way, but I am pleased to note that HQMC now has a full-time Chief of Staff and a full-time Assistant Commandant, and in the long term, I think I was proved right.

I could not have had a better last four years in the Marine Corps. I have more good memories of those four years than my mind can accommodate.

My Second Career:

International Business

On the very morning that I submitted my request to the Secretary of the Navy for retirement from the Marine Corps, I received a courtesy visit in my office from Dr. Nick Yaru, President of the Ground Systems Group, Hughes Aircraft Company. During my time as Director of the Development Center, I had met with Dr. Yaru on matters related to our Marine Corps contracts with his company. At the completion of his visit, he said, "The next time I am in Washington, I would like to visit with you again."

My response was, "On your next visit, Dr. Yaru, I will no longer be in this office. I will share with you that I have just submitted my request for retirement on 31 May. You are the first one to know that, and I ask you not to tell anyone until there is a public news release about it."

He said, "What do you plan to do after retirement?"

I said, "I don't know, because I am not willing to talk about it until I am out of uniform."

He said, "Well, good luck in whatever you decide to do." With that, he departed. I did not give it another thought.

About ten days later, I received a phone call from Dr. Yaru. "I have seen the release about your retirement," he said. "I am calling because our Corporate International Vice President will be in Washington next week, and I have suggested that he invite you to dinner one evening. Would you be receptive to that?"

"Have him call me and we will see what might be feasible," I responded.

Two days later, Mr. George Todd, Hughes Aircraft Company International VP, called and we scheduled a dinner. After dinner, as we enjoyed coffee and dessert, Mr. Todd said that he wanted to talk with me about possibly going to work for Hughes Aircraft Company. He said that the Retired Air Force Brigadier General who managed the Far East area, with primary office in Tokyo, needed to come home, and I was the ideal man to replace him. "Further," said George Todd, "we have checked out your outstanding record in Japan and know that you are who we have been looking for."

With that, he slipped a 3x5 card face down under my dessert plate and said, "This card indicates the compensation and allowances involved. Why don't you discuss this with your wife and, if you are interested in the next step, we will have you come out to Los Angeles for a one-week visit to see the company and meet the Chairman and others who you would work with. We will cover your expenses for the trip. Please call me as soon as you are ready to talk about what we do next."

Martha and I spent the next several days talking about returning to Japan, and we decided to take the next step. So, I spent a full week in Los Angeles, visited each of the Presidents of the Groups of Hughes Aircraft Company, had lunches with them, received extensive briefings by their staffs, and had in-depth discussions about their programs in Japan, Korea, and Taiwan.

On the final day of the Los Angeles trip, I had lunch with the company President John Richardson, Chairman Allen Puckett, Emeritus Chairman Pat Hyland, and several Corporate Staff members. After lunch, I went into John Richardson's office, where he invited me join the Company as Vice President, Far East Area, Hughes Aircraft International Service Company, the organizational part of HAC which handled all international business.

I said, "John, before I accept your offer, I want your personal assurance that in Japan, Korea, and Taiwan, there are no illegal relationships and no money being paid under the table to government officials or others to sell Hughes products or services to their military services. During my time in Tokyo, I heard a number of stories about illicit business practices by American companies in the Far East. After three years in Japan, I left there with my personal integrity intact, and I won't be part of any such practices when I go back there. If I find any such conduct by this company in my area, I will be on the first plane home. Do I have your assurance of that?"

He said, "You have my assurance on that."

I also told John Richardson that I would not market Hughes services or products to U.S. Forces in Japan or in other countries. I said that I did not want to take advantage of my friendships with active-duty military to gain information for the company. That policy on my part turned to an unexpected advantage to me in my three countries. The senior U.S. military officers in my three countries knew that I was not there to market or sell them anything, so I had access to all the senior officers. They did not treat me as a defense contractor but as a fellow General Officer, and I made a lot of new friends in each of our military services which turned out to be most enjoyable.

I added one more condition to my employment arrangement. My replaced left knee was uncomfortable jammed up against the tourist class airline seats, so I told John that my air travel must be all first class because those long flights over the Pacific Ocean were just too uncomfortable for me. He said, "No problem."

Finally, I said to John Richardson, "With those issues settled, I accept you offer of employment, and I look forward to working with you. I will now visit with George Todd and work out the details."

And that is how I went to work for Hughes Aircraft Company.

In the Hughes Aircraft International Service Company (HAISC), Tokyo office, I had a fine staff of five: a retired Army LtCol, a native

Japanese project officer, a *Nisei* Japanese (totally fluent in Japanese), two Japanese women as secretaries, and a Japanese driver. I had highly effective retired Marine Corps Officers as managers of the HAISC offices in Seoul and Taipei. They arranged for me to be treated royally when I visited them on company business. They used my visits as an event to invite ranking military officers and government officials to cocktails and dinners, drawing on my title as Vice President, Far East of HAISC. In the Far East, titles are important both socially and business wise.

There was another bonus to my position in Tokyo.

As Chief of Staff, U.S. Forces, Japan, I wanted the American business community in the Tokyo area to know what our Forces were doing in Japan, why we were there, and how we worked out our problems with the Government of Japan. I had gotten to know George Purdy and his Japanese wife, Midori, very well, so I worked out a plan to have a group of members of the American Chamber of Commerce in Japan (ACCJ) visit Yokota for a full day. I assured them that I would personally brief them, would give them a ride along the 5th Air Force flight line, and have them join the troops for lunch in one of the Mess Halls.

When the day came, there were two large commercial tour buses full of ACCJ members plus several individual carloads of members. It was a first-time event for the ACCJ, and they responded with great enthusiasm. They were impressed that I was their briefer and that I spent the entire day with them. They left in late afternoon, very pleased with the day's program and feeling they had been given a lot of inside info about our military presence in Japan (to include Okinawa, which had just been returned to Japan by the U.S. Government).

The other half of my good fortune in my returning there as a civilian was by my great relationship with senior members of the Japanese government. As Chief of Staff, U.S. Forces, I was the U.S. Co-Chairman of the U.S.-Japan Joint Committee, which was the first place where military base problems and other Mutual Security Treaty were addressed.

I told George that I would take the job for three years, but I stayed in Japan for seven and a half years. Shortly after I told George that I really planned to leave Japan, I received a call from Blaine Shull, President of the Ground Systems Group, asking me to join that Group as Vice President International with an office in Fullerton, California, 20 miles from downtown Los Angeles.

After some short negotiations about salary, I agreed to take the job. I was responsible for Ground Systems Group's programs around the world, but as it turned out, I spent most of my travel time in the Mid-East on programs in Pakistan, Saudi Arabia, Egypt, United Arab Emirates, and other such places. Doing business in the Far East and doing business in the Mid-East required a total reorientation of the "how" of doing business, but it was a unique business experience which I found challenging and fascinating.

While I was in Ground Systems Group, George Todd, the Corporate International Vice President, retired for health reasons and was followed by Dave Snyder who moved up from one of the Groups. Dave was a top-notch golfer and was Club Champion at Bel Air Country Club for several years. He enhanced the Hughes Aircraft Company image among the big wheels in Hollywood and the Los Angeles area.

When Dave died unexpectedly, I was offered the job. I turned it down for two reasons, despite the fact that it would have more than doubled my salary. First of all, I was past the retirement age that the President of GM had established. And second, I was not willing to commute from Fullerton to Marina Del Rey, nor was I willing for Martha to be alone up in that area of Los Angeles so much of the time because of the extensive traveling required by the job.

I told the President that if I could not do what the company wanted me to, it was time for me to go home. And that is the way my time with Hughes ended. I have regretted missing the opportunity to get the big money in the job, but for the good of my family, it was the right decision.

During our time with Hughes Aircraft Company, Martha and I

lived "high on the hog," as the old expression goes. We traveled extensively, always first class, stayed in the finest hotels in Korea and Taiwan, entertained high-level military and government officials at the finest restaurants in Tokyo or wherever we were. This was all sanctioned by my bosses in Los Angeles, who wanted the company to be recognized as a first-class company; and I did what I could to enhance that image. I had an unlimited expense account and had a long-time Japanese secretary who knew how to prepare my expense account without ever being questioned by the corporate staff. I can truthfully say that I never abused the expense account, but often thought that the company was far too generous in that area.

I was in a similar situation as International Vice President for the Ground Systems Group, because one of my functions was to host a lot of the foreign customers who visited the Fullerton plant. I took them to fine restaurants along the coast, including the Queen Mary Cruise Ship and the Spruce Goose aircraft (both side by side in Long Beach) and other notable restaurants with fine wines and outstanding cuisine; cost didn't matter. That explains why my cholesterol level was above 300 when I left the company. In sum, my international business second career was highly successful, very enjoyable, and well rewarded. As I commented in another section of this document, Bob Barrow did a fine job as Commandant, and I went on to a very successful second career. Where there are two winners like that, there is no loser!

Beirut

My first encounter with the Beirut tragedy started one Friday morning while I was working and living in Tokyo. At 0230 on that Friday morning, I answered my bedside telephone to hear the voice on the other end say, "General, this is Major General Colin Powell calling from the Office of the Secretary of Defense."

I said, "Thank you, General Powell, what can I do for you in Tokyo at 2:30 on this Friday morning?"

He said, "The Secretary wants you here in his office Sunday evening for a briefing. You're going to serve on the Commission to investigate the terrorist bombing of the Marine unit in Beirut."

I said, "General Powell, in this part of the world, I go and come as I please, but if I leave the Far East area, I need the approval of my boss back in Los Angeles."

General Powell's response was a classic. He said, "General, I suggest you make immediate flight plans. My boss will take care of your boss."

At that time, my company, Hughes Aircraft Company, was the number one electronic supplier to the Defense Department. Secretary Caspar Weinberger did call my boss, and within an hour, my boss called and said, "Go when and where they want you. Just let me know when you are ready to return to your office. Let Martha go wherever she wants to go; we will take care of her expenses."

You can be sure I was in the Secretary's office at 6:30 that Sunday evening.

Secretary Weinberger made it clear that he wanted a very thorough investigation, starting on the ground in Beirut and all the way back to his office, the CIA, and the FBI. Each of the service chiefs and the Joint Chiefs of Staff had already been told that any request we made to them would receive priority response. We were authorized to review highly classified documents and messages. We were assigned our own special mission aircraft, which took us to Beirut, London, Italy, Spain, Cypress, Israel, Germany, and any other place we needed to go to interview survivors or obtain information.

It is important to understand that the commission was headed by Admiral Bob Long, U.S. Navy, and had a three-star general from the Army, the Air Force, and the Marine Corps and one civilian, a former Under Secretary of the Navy, who jestingly reminded us that he was there to keep us honest about our military affiliation. We had long get-acquainted sessions in which we each pledged to search for the facts without any service favoritism and let the chips fall where they may. And, as military men, we had no concerns about political fallout.

Mine was the hardest task. I was investigating my own Marine Corps, in which I had served more than 37 years of active duty. More than that, Colonel Tim Geraghty, who had overall command of the Beirut unit, had worked for me as a major, and I viewed him as an outstanding Marine. When I first heard about the bombing, I was aware that he was there, and my first concern was for him and his family back home.

Although I will not get into the details of the terrorist attack, or the heroic efforts of the survivors to rescue and evacuate the dead and wounded, I have jotted down a summary of our findings, our conclusions, and our recommendations.

First, we said that the terrorist act was supported by the sovereign states of Iran and Syria, and that our U.S. forces were not trained, equipped, or adequately supported to deal with international terrorism supported by sovereign states.

Second, we said that the "presence mission" for the multi-national force was ill defined and not interpreted the same by all levels of the chain of command.

Third, responsibility of the multi-national force for the security of the Beirut International Airport should have been recognized and corrected by the chain of command.

Fourth, U.S. decisions as regards Lebanon over the prior fifteen months were characterized by emphasis on military options in which the security of the multi-national force was allowed to deteriorate as diplomatic efforts slowed.

Fifth, we urged the National Security Council to re-examine military options and pursue a more vigorous and demanding approach to pursuing diplomatic alternatives.

Sixth, we found that a single set of rules of engagement had not been provided to, nor implemented by, the Marine amphibious unit commander.

Seventh, the mission statement, the rules of engagement, and the different ways of implementing the rules of engagement detracted from the readiness of the USMNF to respond to the threat which materialized on 23 October 1983.

Eighth, the Commission holds the view that military commanders are responsible for the performance of their subordinates. The commander can delegate some or all of his authority to his subordinates, but he cannot delegate his responsibility for the force he commands.

Ninth, the Commission concluded that USCINEUR in Germany, CINCUSNAVEUR in London, COMSIXTHFLEET in Naples, and Commander, Task Force 61, offshore from Lebanon, did not initiate actions to ensure the security of the multi-national force in light of the deteriorating political/military situation in Lebanon.

Tenth, the Commission concluded that the failure of the operational chain of command to correct or amend the defensive posture of the USMNF constituted tacit approval of the large number of men and the security measures in force at the battalion landing team (BLT) Headquarters on 23 October.

Eleventh, the USMNF commander was not provided with the intelligence information as to his specific operational needs that was necessary to defend against the broad spectrum of threats he faced.

Twelfth, the Commission concluded that the BLT commander must take responsibility for the concentration of approximately 350 members of his command in the BLT Headquarters building, thereby providing a lucrative target for the terrorist attack.

Thirteenth, the Commission also concluded that the Marine Amphibious Unit commander shares responsibility for the catastrophic losses in that he condoned the concentration of personnel in the building, concurred in the modification of the alert procedures, and emphasized safety over security in directing that sentries on Posts 4, 5, 6, and 7 would not load their weapons.

As a Commission, it was our view that the catastrophic magnitude of this terrorist event required the best that we could bring to the investigation based on the facts we gathered. It was not a pleasant task, but one that had to be done.

Photo Gallery

TOP LEFT AND RIGHT: My maternal grandparents: Stuart Ryder Huffman and Nora Huffman (later Nora Pitzer).

ABOVE LEFT: This was my father at approximately 18 months. There are no other pictures of him until the one in his riding clothes at the time of his marriage to my mother.

ABOVE RIGHT: My mother, Beatrice Magnolia Huffman, born May 12, 1896. She was approximately two years old in this photo.

TOP LEFT: My father at about the time of his marriage to my mother. The riding outfit was his working uniform when he drove the livery wagons up to Monticello.

TOP RIGHT: My mother, 1940s.

ABOVE LEFT: At age 4 (1925), I sang my first solo in church at the First Baptist Church in Charlottesville, Virginia. The Lord Fauntleroy suit was made of red velvet. My father was in the church choir and my mother was the pianist/organist for the church.

ABOVE RIGHT: Boy Scout, 1935 (age 14).

TOP: McGuffey School, 1931.

ABOVE: The cast of "Miss Blue Eyes." I had the leading role. The girl in the chair in dark dress is Betty Shumate, the leading female. We later became very good friends.

TOP LEFT: As a sophomore at Lane High School, I was selected to be on the cover of the yearbook. I can't explain why.

TOP RIGHT: Virginia Beach - 1940, I believe.

ABOVE: 1938 Charlottesville, Virginia Fox Hunter-Farmington Country Club.

ABOVE LEFT: With my father at Camp Lejeune, NC, 1943 (2nd Lt.).

ABOVE RIGHT: With my mother, about 1942.

RIGHT: My father with "Rocky," about 1942. Rocky was a mixed-breed Collie, born in the attic of a fraternity house at the University of Virginia. Rocky moved to our house on Evergreen Avenue to be my "replacement" when I departed for Marine Corps service. Rocky was a most obedient dog, without any training. In exchange for food and love, he offered total loyalty and sincere love. A great dog!

TOP LEFT: This is my wife, Martha, in 1944. Any time I was overseas, she was a Red Cross volunteer nurse's aide, bandage roller, and baker of cookies and candies to send to the troops overseas.

TOP RIGHT: Honolulu, late 1944 before loading out for Iwo Jima - Rank of Captain.

ABOVE LEFT: At our tent camp on Maui, Hawaii, 1944.

ABOVE RIGHT: Officers and senior NCOs of K Company. I am the only officer survivor.

TOP: 1940s Foxhole (L-R): Company Gunnery Sergeant Harold Douglas, Snowden, 1st Lt Charles Ahearn.

ABOVE LEFT: 1940s Fox Company 23rd Marine Regiment (L-R): 1st Lt. Company Executive Officer Charles Ahearn; Snowden; 1st Lt. Frank Collins, Platoon Leader.

ABOVE RIGHT: Received Masters Degree from Northwestern University, Evanston, Ill. June 1950 (age 29).

ABOVE: I am up on the stage facing to my right as the Announcer/Narrator for the birthday ceremony and the cake-cutting. The officer in front of me on the main floor is the guest of honor, General Lauris Norstad, U.S. Air Force, Supreme Allied Commander, Europe.

LEFT: Lt. Colonel, Camp Pendleton; Chairman, Base Stables Committee, 1961. I was Chairman of the Hunt at Pendleton (as well as at Quantico) and organized the junior fox hunt.

TOP: This photo was taken in the 1960s. (L-R): Son Brian; Gen. Leonard Chapman, Commandant, Marine Corps; wife Martha; Snowden; my mother Beatrice.

ABOVE LEFT: John Stephen, Beatrice, Snowden in 1964 when I was commissioned.

ABOVE RIGHT: October 20, 1966: Roy Rogers and Dale Evans visited the troops in Chu Lai, Vietnam. I presented them with the Regimental Certificate of Appreciation.

TOP: Being presented a Letter of Appreciation by Brigadier General Kim, 20 January 1967.

ABOVE LEFT: Colonel, 06 June 1968.

ABOVE RIGHT: Commandant General Leonard F. Chapman presenting my personal Brigadier General Officer flag, 1968.

TOP LEFT: Brigadier General, 08 April 1969.

TOP RIGHT: Lieutenant General, 14 June 1977.

ABOVE LEFT: Chief of Staff - US Forces Japan, 1972-1975.

ABOVE RIGHT: Martha in 1974.

TOP: President and Mrs. Jimmy Carter greeting Martha and me, approx. 1976.

ABOVE: Joint Chiefs of Staff (JCS) with their operation deputies standing behind. Front
row (L-R): Bernard Rogers, U.S. Army; Jim Holloway, U.S. Navy; George Brown,
Chair-man, JCS; David Jones, U.S. Air Force; Lou Wilson, U.S. Marine Corps.
Back row (L-R): Eugene Meyer, U.S. Army; Jim Moorer, U.S. Navy; Ray Sitton,
Assistant Chairman, JCS; Any Anderson, Jr., U.S. Air Force; Snowden, U.S.
Marine Corps. Photo @1977, signed by the Joint Chiefs and their deputies.

LEFT: Final appearance in uniform as an active duty Marine. Marine Corps Barracks, Washington, DC, 31 May 1979.

BELOW: In May 1979, after my retirement became public knowledge, I received a query about going down to the Citadel to be interviewed for the position of President of the University. Photos of the President's quarters, including the one below, were sent to entice me. I gracefully declined.

As president of the American Chamber of Commerce in Japan, I hosted several celebrities, including Jack Nicklaus, with whom I played a round of golf. He gave me an autographed golf glove, which I gave to my great-grandson several years ago. (He happens to be a pretty good golfer.)

TOP LEFT AND RIGHT: President, American Chamber of Commerce in Japan, 1982.

ABOVE LEFT & RIGHT: Covers of the Journal of the American Chamber of Commerce in Japan, 1982 and 1983. Used by permission of ACCJ.

TOP: Testifying to U.S. Senate Budget Committee re: US-Japan friction, approx. 1985. Senator John Danforth headed the committee.

ABOVE: In 1986, discussing the U.S.-Japan fair trade issue with Mike Mansfield, U.S. Ambassador to Japan. Mansfield served as U.S. Senator from Montana and was a proud Marine.

TOP: Emperor (then Crown Prince) Akihito and Princess Michiko arrive at the Tokyo Club, circa 1987.

ABOVE: As the guest of honor at the Sunset Parade, I had the honor to speak with Japanese Ambassador Ichiro Fujisaki during the reception at the Women in Military Service for America Memorial at Arlington National Cemetery. U.S. Marine Corps photo by Sgt. Christopher A. Green, 03 July 2012.

TOP: (L-R): Florida State Comptroller Gerald Lewis, Secretary of State Jim Smith, Governor Lawton Chiles, Attorney General Bob Butterworth, State Representative Tom Gallagher, Education Secretary Betty Castor, Snowden, unidentified woman, and Department of Elder Affairs Deputy Secretary June Noel. Inscription by Gov. Chiles reads, "To my good friend Larry. Thank you for all of your help and support. Lawton."

ABOVE: Yasunori Nishi, left, and retired Marine Lt. Gen. Lawrence F. Snowden hold an old Japanese flag during the 67th Iwo Jima Reunion of Honor ceremony, 14 March 2012. Photo by Lance Cpl. Alyssa N. Hoffacker.

TOP: With Diet Member Yoshitaka Shindo, grandson of Lt. Gen. Tadamichi Kuribayashi, commander of the Japanese forces on Iwo Jima; Akie Abe, wife of Japanese Prime Minister Shinzō Abe; and Caroline Kennedy, U.S. Ambassador to Japan, during PM Abe's address to a Joint Session of Congress, 29 April 2015. (Kenichiro Sasae, Japanese Ambassador to the United States, wrote the inscription on the photo when he visited me in Tallahassee on 13 Nov. 2015.)

ABOVE: At the monument on Mount Siribachi for the 70th Anniversary of Iwo Jima, 2015 (L-R): Officer of IJAA Lt. Gen. Norman Smith, USMC Ret., President of IJAA; Lt. Gen. Hank Stackpole, Chairman, IJAA; Col. Warren Wiedhahn, USMC Ret., President, Military Historical Tours, Executive Secretary of IJAA; Snowden.

TOP LEFT: 70th Anniversary Reunion of Honor, Iwo Jima, 2015.

TOP RIGHT: 4th Marine Division Reunion, 2014.

ABOVE: Reception at Governor's Mansion after induction into Florida Veterans Hall of Fame, 2015. (L-R): Gov. Rick Scott, Florida First Lady Ann Scott, Snowden, Beverly Ewald.

TOP LEFT: I bought Starter Kit ("Sunny"), AQHA-Registered Quarter Horse, in 1995 when she was 15 years old. Sunny served extremely well as a gentle, lovable horse that helped me develop my legs for riding again.

TOP RIGHT: AQHA-registered Quarter Horse Blue Rebel. As a Novice team, "Blue" and I won 7 Blues (1st), 9 Reds (2nd), 10 Yellows (3rd), 8 Whites (4th), 5 Pinks (5th), and 3 Greens (6th). In our only Senior Division effort, we won 1 Blue, 1 Red, 2 Yellow, 1 Pink, and 1 Green. (1995-1997)

ABOVE LEFT: AQHA-registered Quarter Horse gelding, Southern by Design ("Rusty").

TOP RIGHT: Corval Cinnamon Ravenhurst, CD. "Cindy" was our third and last Corgi.

TOP: Japanese Ambassador Kenichiro Sasae presents me with a bronze eagle head, Nov. 2015.

ABOVE: My dear friend Ken Sasae poses with me in Tallahassee, Nov. 2015.

TOP LEFT: Medals received on 18 March 2016: Department of the Navy Distinguished Public Service Award (left) and Department of Defense Medal for Distinguished Public Service (right), presented by General Robert B. Neller, Commandant of the U.S. Marine Corps.

TOP RIGHT: Certificate from the Department of the Defense, presented by Commandant Neller at the Awards Ceremony.

ABOVE: A private moment with General Neller prior to the awards ceremony, 18 March 2016.

Photos this page ©M.R. Street.

TOP: With George and Wanda Fong at the Awards Ceremony in Tallahassee, 18 March 2016.

ABOVE: Marine veterans stand with Commandant Neller at the Awards Ceremony, 18 March 2016. Photo ©W. George Fong. Used with permission.

TOP LEFT: My sons, John Stephen and Brian, at the Awards Ceremony in Tallahassee, 18 March 2016. Photo ©W. George Fong. Used with permission.

TOP RIGHT: Brigadier General William Webb, US Air Force (Ret.); Snowden; Commander Dennis Baker, US Navy (Ret.). Photo by Norma Jean Baker. Used with permission.

ABOVE: Lieutenant General Lawrence F. Snowden, US Marine Corps (Ret.). (U.S. Marine Corps Photo)

My Third and Final Career:

Volunteering in Tallahassee

After I had submitted my retirement request to the President of the Ground Systems Group of Hughes Aircraft Company, my focus turned to where Martha and I would live in our retirement years. Her first consideration was to return to our hometown of Charlottesville, Virginia. I said, "Martha, if we decide on Charlottesville, when we get there, I am going to buy you the best snow shovel that I can find and when the snow arrives, it is over to you, lady. Men die from heart attacks shoveling snow, but women usually do not. I don't think we want to go there. The town has grown so much, it is no longer the town we grew up in, so let's look at other possibilities."

Steve was still an active-duty Marine and Brian had moved to Tallahassee, Florida, to work for an international paper company with headquarters in Quincy, Florida, just 26 miles west of Tallahassee. I had not seen Brian for more than a year, so I made a weekend trip to Tallahassee. Brian lived in Killearn Estates in a modest little house, and he and Julia were very enthusiastic about living in Tallahassee. Brian drove me around the area, and as we drove down McLaughlin Drive and passed an empty lot, I told Brian that if I ever lived in Tallahassee, that is where I would like to live, never believing at that time that we would ever live there.

One year later, I decided to visit Tallahassee again and decide whether we wanted to consider Tallahassee as our retirement home. So I made another quick weekend trip. By then, Mary Jane and Bob Allen had moved to Tallahassee from Miami, where Bob had been a dean at the University of Miami. I stayed with them, but again, Brian drove me and a real estate agent (Beverly Green) around the area, looking at potential houses to buy.

When we turned down McLaughlin Drive, I immediately remembered the vacant lot that I liked so much, and there stood Mr. Charles Phillips, the builder, as workers were pouring the concrete footing for a house. Charlie said he was building for sale and showed me the architectural plans for the house, an Alpine-chalet style house. I asked if he was willing to change the appearance and some inside changes, and his answer was, "I will change anything you want, provided I do not have to go back downtown for another permit." Tallahassee still has a notorious reputation for a tough, slow permitting process.

I took a copy of the plans over to Mary Jane's and stayed up until 2 a.m., noting changes I would like to make. I identified sixteen changes I thought would be good and provided the list to Charlie at 7:30 the next morning. He accepted all but four of them, so I said, "I will get back to California and discuss the situation with my wife. But I will tell you now that I want the house with the changes you have accepted. When I have my wife's approval, I will mail you the down payment, and that will be no later than next week."

He said, "We have a deal." And so we had our house and moved into it in September 1988.

As soon as we were in our house, I received a call from Colonel Bill Wier, USMC, Retired, a resident of Killearn Estates, inviting me to have lunch with several other retired Marine officers at the old Brown Derby Restaurant, a long-established watering hole for lots of folks. The Marine group had previously met there for lunch on Mondays, but the schedule had just faded away. Bill said, "Now that you are here, maybe we can get the Monday group back together." We did just that, and even now, the Retired Marine Officer Monday Lunch Bunch meets regularly after our renewed start in 1988.

Again, soon after our arrival, I learned that the wife of a retired New York City detective, now a resident in the Killearn area, had a Welsh Corgi that was expecting a litter. Having previously experienced owning a Corgi, I called on the woman, and she said I could have first choice of the litter. So in a couple of weeks, we had our second Corgi, whom we named Mandy.

When Mandy was three months old, I entered her in a puppy class in the lobby of my veterinarian, Dr. Gaea Mitchell. The class was just for socialization with other dogs, but it got me back into the dog-training frame of mind, so I joined the Tallahassee Dog Obedience Club, trained Mandy through her first title as a Companion Dog (CD), became an assistant instructor, and after five years, became a senior instructor.

When Mandy was about age 12 or so, we lost her to stomach cancer. I found another Corgi (Cindy) down in Chiefland, Florida, and went through the training with her to CD. She had a broken shoulder at the age of one, and I chose not to pursue her Companion Dog Excellent (CDX) because jumping was painful for her. A couple of years after Martha's death, I relocated Cindy to a beautiful home outside of Atlanta with a woman who gave her tons of affection and great care.

After attending several local horse shows, I decided that I wanted to ride again. I was more or less around horses from the time I was in high school. I had always been an English-style rider, but decided it was time to shift to Western-style riding, so I started looking for a Quarter Horse. I joined the Leon County Horsemen's Association, and over time, I became Vice President of the Association. I owned and showed three very nice Quarter Horses; each of them had national registry papers in the American Quarter Horse Association.

I won a few blue ribbons, but was usually outclassed by riders who were fifty years or so younger than I was. They all loved to beat the General, and that was ok with me. I rode for exercise, competition, and fun, and the rest of it didn't matter. I kept my horses at Happy Trails Ranch, the stables of Nicki Francis, a young divorcee who owned thirteen acres and a nice barn, taught Western riding, and ran summer riding camps. We became life-long friends.

A friend invited me to a luncheon program put on by the Economic Club of Florida. I enjoyed the speaker and the lunch, so my friend sponsored me for membership. I was a very regular attendee, and after a couple of years, I was invited to speak at one of the luncheon programs and to talk about Iwo Jima. I resisted that idea at first, insisting that the membership was interested in economic issues and would not be interested in hearing about a WWII battle. I was totally wrong. There was a huge crowd, and I guess I put on one of my best performances, because no one left until I stopped answering questions.

When I spoke about hand-to-hand combat by my eighteen-year-old Marines, I pulled out my Marine K-bar knife. Holding it high, I said that some Marines were alive today because they knew how to use this weapon in kill-or-be-killed situations. The total silence at that moment was overwhelming; the only sound was several women crying. It has been remarkable over the years how many people remember that moment and speak to me about it.

I was elected Vice President and then President of the club, and in 2012 became Chairman of the Board of Directors. I was honored by the club in 2007 by being named Distinguished Floridian of the Year for my lifetime accomplishments. The club presented me with two hand-carved marble eagle heads, which I display with great pride in my apartment at Westminster Oaks.

When Lawton Chiles was running for governor of the State of Florida, he promised to establish a Department of Elder Affairs where he would consolidate all federal and state programs which had to do with helping the state's many senior citizens. My initial reaction was that he was throwing a political bone to the many senior citizens in Florida, but when I learned that he had already hired an executive secretary to run the new department, I knew he was serious – and he truly was. When Bentley Lipscomb, Secretary Designate of the new agency, spoke to a small group of us at a breakfast meeting, I learned that the Governor had big plans. Lipscomb had a ton of work to do and only a small group of folks doing the work, so I volunteered to assist him in any way that I could. When I first visited him in his temporary office, he offered me an office, a desk, and a telephone; I declined. I said, "Mr. Secretary, I want to help in any way that I can, but I prefer to take on individual assignments or projects, and I will work at home. But I will be here any time you want me here. I want to be a full member of your team, but would like to report directly to you."

He replied, "That's our deal." And so it was.

Governor Chiles had just appointed an eight-person advisory board for the department, and my first assignment was to write a speech for board members to use when they spoke to civic groups about the role of the new department. We wanted each of them to deliver the same message as to what the department was going to do. Later, as part of a three-person team, we visited a number of local stores to educate their sales staff about the problems of senior customers who had poor hearing or poor visibility and could not read the fine print on labels and could not communicate easily with the sales staff. We offered to train the trainers. Later, as part of a three-person team, I traveled around the state to help establish and train three AmeriCorps units on how to work with older citizens in their homes and deal with their frailties.

Shortly after my arrival in Tallahassee, I started singing in the choir of Celebration Baptist Church. I continued to do so for the next twenty-two years. When I was diagnosed with bronchiectasis, I lost all my vocal qualities, have not sung a note since 2007, and never will again. My doctor told me that the good news was that the condition would not kill me, but the bad news was that the condition cannot be cured. I get lots of inquiries about why I no longer sing, and I get lots of nice comments about my singing days, but I just tell the truth with great sorrow on my part. Singing played a major role in my life, and I miss it dreadfully, but I accept it as God's will and get on with my life, grateful for the fine talent I had for so long.

Personal Anecdotes

There are a number of instances in my life which I recall with great joy, instances in which I was interacting with some of the "giants" of the Marine Corps. These events will not be in chronological order but will be recorded here as I happen to think of them.

The Pool of Potential "Giants"

My first tour of duty at HQMC was from June 1946 to June 1949. During that time, I had the good fortune to work with a number of officers who became, in my view, "giants" of the Corps. Over those three years, I worked very closely with the following:

- Then Brigadier General Gerald C. Thomas, later retired as General, Assistant Commandant
- Then Colonel David M. Shoup, later Commandant*
- Then Colonel Fred Weissman, later Lieutenant General*
- Then Colonel Wallace M. Greene, Jr., later Commandant
- Then LtCol Leonard Chapman, later Commandant
- Then LtCol Rathvon McC. Tompkins, later Major General*
- Then Major Louis Metzger, later Lieutenant General*
- Then LtCol John Wermuth, later Brigadier General, USMCR*
- Then Colonel Harvey Tschirgi, later Brigadier General*
- Then LtCol Alvin S. Sanders, later Brigadier General*

*These officers were my fellow workers in the G-4 Section. Allowing as how I made it to Lieutenant General, I would say that particular Section was loaded with potential giants (though I never felt that I ranked with those giants)!

My Memorable Moments with the Legendary

Quartermaster General

During that first HQMC tour, I had a memorable personal experience with Major General W. P. T. Hill, the Quartermaster General of the Marine Corps. General Hill was a unique Marine who managed to earn two Master's Degrees while serving in the Corps. He was the primary presenter of the Marine Corps budget to the Congress, where he became a favorite Service witness. Because of the reputation of the Marine Corps for being a very frugal Service, and because he had a personal reputation for being an honest bookkeeper, General Hill, after presentation of the Marine Corps budget, was often asked if he was sure that was all the funding the Marine Corps required. On several occasions when asked if the Corps could use more funds than requested, General Hill reportedly responded, "When we need it, I will ask for it."

He was one of the "darlings" of the Congress.

Colonel Shoup and General Hill were constantly at odds over budget matters. In the late 1940s, the Quartermaster General was the budget keeper, and a lot of budget information was kept in a little green notebook that General Hill kept in his right rear trouser pocket. That alone was distressing to Colonel Shoup, but the pot boiled over when the Quartermaster General would say that he agreed to the need for some item but "there is no money available for it."

It was Colonel Shoup's position that it was a decision by the Commandant about how money was to be spent, and the Quartermaster General was only the bookkeeper.

I think the year was 1947, and the item in question was a new type of field jacket for the troops. The G-4 proposed buying the field jackets and prepared the appropriate staff paper to go up to the Commandant for decision. The proposal had to be sent around the staff for coordination and concurrence. Every office concurred with the idea, and the only office left to initial the paper was the Quartermaster General.

One mid-morning, Colonel Shoup asked me to take the paper up to General Hill for his "chop" (initials on the routing sheet). Colonel Shoup said, "General Hill will be waiting for you."

I went up to his second floor office, and his secretary said, "The General is expecting you." I knocked on the closed door, opened it, and walked up to his desk. I stood rigidly at attention, waiting for him to acknowledge my presence.

General Hill sat at his desk, the large window behind him looking out over a part of Arlington National Cemetery. The General was wearing his half glasses and was intensely reading a document. Without looking up, he asked, "Is this the paper from Colonel Shoup?"

I said, "Yes, Sir, it is, and he said that I should wait for it."

As I handed him the paper, a military funeral was underway just a short distance into the cemetery, and the 21-volley salute was loud and clear. With that, he turned around in his chair and looked out the window at the funeral site. After a moment, he turned back my way, initialed the routing sheet, and added a few words in the comment box. As he handed me the paper, he looked at me over his granny glasses and said, "I'm not going to let them bury me over there. I wouldn't be cold in the ground before some young Captain would be out there asking for my initial on a staff paper."

I said, "Thank you, sir," did an about face, and departed his office. End of the story? Not quite!

General Hill had initialed his agreement with the need for the field jacket, but then wrote in the Comment box, "No money is available for this item."

When I handed the paper to Colonel Shoup, his response was in language which I will not record here. He then proceeded to tell me again how the Quartermaster General thought he was the decision-maker on budget matters when it fact his only job was to keep the books. Colonel Shoup vowed at that time that he was going to change the way budget decisions were made, insure that the decisions were made by the

Commandant and not by "some blankety-blank staff officer."

Now for the end of the story. Later, Brigadier General Shoup persuaded the Commandant to establish the office of Fiscal Director with responsibility for compiling the budget and maintaining all the records pertaining to the budget. And who was the first Fiscal Officer? David Monroe Shoup! The Fiscal Director position endures today, but for a number of years now the billet has been filled by a civilian, usually at the GS-18 level.

The Iwo Zero

Iwo Jima provided a unique experience which will be forever in my personal memory bank. It was D-Day plus two or three. My company (Fox Company, 2nd Battalion, 23rd Marines, 4th Marine Division) was on the edge of the first airfield (Motoyama #1) late in the afternoon. A number of Japanese Zero fighter planes had come down from Chi Chi Jima to attack our ships. From my foxhole position, I had a front-row seat to see a swarm of Zeros attacking our ships. I saw airplanes crash into the sea, and lots of anti-aircraft fire exploding in the air, a most memorable event. After thirty minutes or so, the Zeros decided to break it off and return to Chi Chi Jima. Not wanting to land back home with a lot of bombs and other ordnance on board, most of the pilots dumped their remaining ordnance and fired their machine guns to get rid of those explosives for safety on landing and to get better fuel distance with a lighter load.

Within a few moments, I could see that one of the Zeros was headed straight for our beach and was directly in line with my position. In those days, the machine guns in the Zeros were fixed in position, and the pilot would raise or dip the nose of the aircraft to put the machine gun fire where he wanted it. Coming in very low and at top speed, his first couple of machine gun bursts hit in the water and then about one hundred yards in from the beach. By the time of his third burst, the rounds were all hitting past my position and up on the airfield runway. I knew I was safe from his fire, so I stood up in my foxhole to get a better look at the Zero. As he crossed the beach and headed for my position, he was off to my left as I faced him. Flying at top speed and at about one hundred feet above the ground, I could see his face quite clearly, with his leather flying helmet and wide glasses. I looked squarely at him and waved. He looked back at me, smiled, nodded, and flew on by, pulling up sharply to his right and headed back to Chi Chi Jima. End of this story? I believe so, but the Japanese did try to add another chapter, as follows.

While serving as Chief of Staff, U.S. Forces, Japan, in Tokyo (first at Fuchu Air Station and later at Yokota Air Force Base), I went down to southern Kyushu to visit a Ground Self Defense Force (Army) Division. The Army Base included a museum which had a mint condition Zero fighter on display. I was standing on the wing of the Zero, looking into the cockpit, when I remembered that Iwo Jima incident. I told that story to the group accompanying me, which included a Vice Admiral (Maritime Self Defense Force –Navy) from the Joint Staff Council and several GSDF Generals.

The Admiral said, "We will find that pilot and get him together with you." He turned to the group and, in Japanese, instructed them to put a team together to conduct the search.

About six months later, the Admiral told me that the research group had no success, and he deeply regretted that they had failed. It was no consolation to him that I commented that it was highly unlikely that any pilot based on Chi Chi Jima survived the war. When we captured the airfields on Iwo Jima, that spelled the end for the Chi Chi Jima base and all the fighters stationed there. Considering how much time has now passed, I am sure that the story is finished.

On Becoming a Marine Corps General Officer

Throughout my twelve years of service as a General Officer I was often asked, "How do you get to be a General in the Marine Corps?"

Usually my short answer was, "Good, clean living and a lot of luck." That usually got rid of the question.

In more serious discussions with younger officers who posed that same question, the flippant answer was not adequate. My broader response to the question had to include issues which they could ponder as they faced future selection boards. I never dropped the need for a "lot of luck," but I underscored that issue by adding two of my favorite personal homilies: "The harder I work, the luckier I get," and, "You can make your own good luck."

Colonels, more than any other group, not being selected for promotion, would often say that they were not selected because they "didn't know any General on the Selection Board."

My response to that statement was, "Who you know on the Board does not matter much. The important issue is, who on that Board has seen you perform, particularly in a high-stress situation? Have you served under any of the Generals on the Board and, if so, did you give them some reason for remembering you and give them some reason to fight for you against a lot of first class competition?"

Further, I would add, "Do your fitness reports provide evidence that you have potential for success at the next higher rank?" Remember, the Board does not select for promotion as a reward for past service; the Board is charged with selecting officers based on their potential for handling greater responsibilities at the higher rank.

Lastly, "Did any of your reporting seniors use words that suggested that you were a cut above the rest of the group being rated, and did any of them indicate that they would want you to serve with them again?"

It was not until after my retirement that I did a thorough review of all my Fitness Reports, and I am pleased that I found evidence that supported my views above. I believe that, because I had several reporting seniors who took the time and made the effort to describe me in terms which set me a notch above the other officers being reported on, I was selected by every Selection Board which I faced and reached the position as one of the top three officers in the Marine Corps in my final four years of active duty service. I do not believe that would have happened if I had not rather consistently been rated as above other fine officers being considered for promotion.

Below, I will list some excerpts from my Fitness Reports, starting back when I was a Captain and on through my time as a Lieutenant General. These excerpts are chosen because they support my ideas about what it takes to come out ahead when you are competing against a large number of officers, most of whom had roughly the same amount of service, had received fitness reports from roughly the same number of reporting seniors, and had served in a variety of different billets.

Reporting Senior: Colonel James A. Tinsley, USMCR, CO, 9th Marine Regiment

> "This Captain, without previous experience and on very short notice, took over position as Regimental S-1, Troop Adjutant and Troop Commander, performed his duties in an outstanding manner. The undersigned is of the opinion that he is the outstanding officer of his rank in the Marine Corps."

> (Wow! There were thousands of Captains at that time!)

Reporting Senior: Colonel David M. Shoup, G-4, Plans and Policies, HQMC

> "He has tackled a new type of job with amazing success."

Reporting Senior: Colonel Henry R. Paige, President, Tactics and Techniques Board, MC Development Center

> "This Major is one of the most efficient officers with whom it has been my pleasure to serve. Recommended for promotion."

> (I had been promoted to Major just a few months before!)

Reporting Senior: Colonel Earl Sneeringer, G-4, 1stMarDiv in Korea

> "He is, without reservation, one of the most outstanding Majors I have served with."

<u>Reporting Senior: Colonel Al Creel, USMC, Director, 1st Marine Corps Recruiting District</u>

(I had the Recruiting Station in New York City.)

"His Station has exceeded assigned quotas indicating his high efficiency and performance. It is a pleasure serving with an officer of his high caliber."

<u>Colonel M. M. Day, Director, Senior School, Quantico, VA.</u>

"It is difficult to overstate the ability of this officer. He is completely confident and a perfectionist in everything he undertakes. A truly fine Marine."

<u>Colonel Russell Duncan, Deputy G-3, HQMC</u>

"The finest staff officer who has ever worked under my supervision and I consider his potentialities for any assignment, command or staff, to be outstanding. I cannot praise his work too highly."

Brigadier Louis Hudson, the G-3, as the Reviewing Officer of the report, added in his own handwriting "Concur strongly in the 'Outstanding" marks." He also added a sheet of paper on which he wrote, "Of the 14 'action officers' I have personally observed briefing the CMC on JCS and strategic planning matters, I have noted the outstanding clarity, completeness, and logical reasoning of this officer's presentations and work. I heartily concur in the remarks concerning the competence and prospective future value to the Marine Corps of this officer's work."

<u>Colonel Sidney Altman, CO, 1st Marine Regiment, 1st Marine Division</u>

(I was Battalion Commander, 3rd Battalion and had been through a training cycle to prepare for rotational deployment to Okinawa. In the final week of that cycle, the Battalion was inspected by Major General Herman Nickerson, CG of the 1st Division. He rated my Battalion as the "most ready" in the Division.)

> "Led his Battalion through a complex training cycle, to include actual mount-out for the Cuban missile crisis. Demonstrated that he is a polished, dynamic, firm, and tactful leader."

Colonel Altman attached to my Fitness Report another Fitness Report prepared by Captain Michael J. Harmon, the Commanding Officer of the USS Iwo Jima, the helicopter carrier which transported my Battalion and a helicopter squadron (under my command) to Cuba via the Panama Canal. That Ship Captain was not required to prepare a report on me but did so, telling Colonel Altman that my "superior performance of duty while aboard his ship deserved to be included in the record."

Captain Michael J. Harmon

> "A thoroughly outstanding officer when judged by any basis. His initiative, judgment, and cooperation left nothing to be desired. I would be delighted to serve with him again under any circumstances."

Lieutenant General Victor H. Krulak, CG, Fleet Marine Force, Pacific

General Krulak was truly one of the "giants" of the Corps and it was a complete mystery to many that he did not become the Commandant. "Vertically challenged," he was short in physical stature (always referred to as Brute) but a giant in every other aspect of his Marine service. He was controversial in many ways, but those of us who were privileged to work with him soon learned of his great personal concern for his troops, and also learned that he was dedicated to "getting it right" the first time. Typical of his philosophy was a small sign on his office door which read, "In this office you can express any opinion you wish, just be sure your facts are correct." (Most of this is already included and the rest should be moved to that section)

> "A distinguished officer, out of the top-most drawer. He is both intelligent and wise. He is strong, resolute, articulate, and logical. Everything he does is done with a degree of thoroughness and polish that is rarely encountered. His growth potential is very

great. I would actively seek his services."

On my departure from FMF PAC, headed for Vietnam, General Krulak's final report read, in part:

> "My views of his competence have not changed. He is a superior officer in every way. He gets stronger, more broadly competent every day. I regard him as one of the three best officers, rank disregarded, in this headquarters. He leaves a vast void, and I will actively seek his services again. Growth potential unlimited."

Because General Krulak was such a giant in the Corps during his time, and had the reputation of being a "hard marker" on fitness reports, I firmly believe that those very favorable reports by him were of great importance to Selection Boards. In the final year of my career, when I was said to be the major competition against Bob Barrow to become Commandant, I am confident that he gave his support to Bob Barrow who had worked even more closely with him than I had. I am still grateful to General Krulak for all the support he gave me.

What conclusions do I draw from all of the above?

First, I was fortunate to serve under several real giants of the Corps, and some of those Reporting Seniors had taken the time and made the effort to set me a notch above most of the other fine officers against whom I was competing for promotion.

Second, several of my reporting seniors (Krulak, Sneeringer, Day, Shoup) had reputations as "hard markers," and their very favorable comments on my performance of duty took on a special meaning.

Third, as a lieutenant colonel working for Brigadier General Cushman, the G-3, HQMC (later Commandant), I was the HQMC authority on the Marine Corps relationship with the Joint Chiefs of Staff (the Commandant was not a Member of the JCS at that time), authority on the Marine Corps relationship with the Navy and as a separate Service within the Department of the Navy and on several other areas of command relationships with the CINC's (CINCPAC, CINCEUR, etc.). That brought me into direct relationship with many of our Generals and gave me exposure not otherwise possible for most of the other Staff Officers. My areas of expertise meant that I spent more time with the Chief of Staff (Lieutenant General Wallace M. Green, Jr., later Commandant) and the Commandant (General Shoup) than did some of the Generals at HQMC, and that did not go unnoticed. That is part of the "good luck" I referred to.

Fourth, and finally, there was not the first shred of any "unfavorable matter" in my records that would give a Selection Board an opportunity to pass me by with very little discussion. On the other hand, several very favorable reports, not part of the fitness reports, were in my record to further boost my stock. For example, Major General Jim Masters wrote a Memo for Record in which he reported that Senior Navy Officials and several Members of Congress had commented most favorably on my performance as a briefer on a team of Navy/Marine Corps officers who briefed newly elected Senators and Congressmen on Department of Defense issues as they began their Congressional service.

It is time to admit that, in my various billets, I was a workaholic. I was always in my office early and was never eager to leave the office just because it was the end of normal office hours. I rarely used leave that was earned and was always available to take the duty on holidays and weekends when no else wanted to get stuck with it. My job was my avocation, my hobby and my "daily bread," and I loved every job I ever had. There were times when I might have been accused of neglecting my family, but that was never a serious issue with my very supportive wife; and besides, my basic philosophy was that the better I did my job, the better opportunity I would have to move up in the Marine Corps, and, if I could keep going up in the Corps, it would be of benefit to my family. Right or wrong, that is the way it was for my 37-plus years of service in the Marine Corps.

Our Small, Small World

Any time you are a long way from home and meet someone from your hometown, one or the other of you is just bound to say, "Boy! It sure is a small world, isn't it?" Most service members have had the enjoyable experience of bumping into a hometown friend or unknown neighbor in some unexpected, faraway place, but my own experience during the Iwo Jima campaign in 1945 still makes me shake my head when I think about it, even though many years have now gone by.

I was a rifle company commander in the Fourth Marine Division during the landing at Iwo on 19 February 1945. On the seventh day ashore, I was caught in the middle of two exploding Japanese artillery shells and suffered severe blast concussion. The next think I remembered was when I came to aboard a Navy hospital ship. A pretty Navy nurse was sitting on the edge of my bunk, writing down my name, religion, and other data from my dog tags. She asked me several questions, including the name of my hometown. When I said I was from Charlottesville, Virginia, she said, "Oh, really?" and broke out in her very biggest smile. She gave me a pill to put me back to sleep and moved on; there were many others to be looked after. As I closed my eyes, I said to myself, "She certainly looks like somebody I know."

The next day, after the doctor had made his rounds, the nurse came back to see me. "Sorry we couldn't talk yesterday, but I was too busy and you were too sick. Didn't you go to the University of Virginia? I went to nursing school there." So that's where I had seen her! In addition to going to school, I used to work with a dance band that played for dances at the university, and I had seen this girl at a number of the medical school dances. I assure you she was pretty enough to be noticed and remembered. After a long discussion about the university and a number of mutual friends, she said, "I'm sure you know Tom Carruthers. I saw him in Noumea a few weeks ago and he gave me some copies of the Daily Progress (the hometown paper), and I'll bring them down to you. My roommate here on the ship is also a graduate of the university nursing school, but we have finished with these papers already, so you may keep them." She brought me about a dozen copies of the Progress. I picked up the top paper, opened it to the page I knew would have all the local news, and the very first picture I saw was one of me, taken when I received my promotion to Captain. My thorough reading of the papers and the daily visits from my nurse friends really boosted my morale and helped pass the long days between Iwo and Guam – our destination.

The hospital ship arrived at Guam a few days later, and most of us were transferred ashore to Fleet Hospital #103. I had been bedded down in the ward only a few minutes when the ward nurse came by to record my personal data again. The usual questions about next of kin and home address disclosed for her that I was from Charlottesville. "Oh," she said, "the doctor I just worked for was from there. Did you ever know a Dr. John Hill or any of the Hill family?" Know them? Ever since I was a small boy! Dr. John Hill's brother Bill was living right next door to my wife and my mother at that very minute. Naturally, this led to discussions about Virginia, Marines, and other Navy people, and we soon discovered mutual friends. Already, the world seemed smaller.

After a few days in the hospital with that good Navy care, there were four of us Marine officers who thought we were ready to go back to our units at Iwo. The doctor was a sympathetic guy who was soon tired of our steady harassment about being discharged from the hospital. He agreed to discharge the four of us to duty provided we could get orders back to our units. He gave three of us liberty from the hospital so we could go to the Advance Headquarters of Fleet Marine Force, Pacific, a few miles up the island, to try for the necessary orders.

Unable to beg any transportation from the hospital motor pool, we walked out to the front gate of the hospital, figuring we should be able to catch a ride if we waited long enough. The very first jeep that came along stopped and offered us a lift. The driver was a Marine lieutenant. As I climbed into the back seat of the jeep, I thought to myself that the lieutenant looked familiar. As we drove on up the road, I noticed that he kept stealing glances at me through his rear view mirror. Finally, I said, "Lieutenant, haven't we met somewhere before?" "Yes, we have," he said. "And it just came to me where it was." As he and I talked of old school days and mutual friends, one of the other officers commented about what a small world it was. But wait –

Assuming that the lieutenant was stationed on Guam, I asked him if he knew where a certain Marine anti-aircraft artillery unit was located on the island. I explained that I had heard that one of my cousins was with that unit. Strangely enough, it turned out to be the same outfit to which the lieutenant belonged, and my cousin was a member of the lieutenant's section! This caused a detour in our trip in order that we could all go by and pay a fast visit to my cousin, who expressed surprise at seeing me there and said something about the fact that the world wasn't so big after all!

The officers at the AAA outfit told us it wasn't going to be easy to get those orders back to Iwo because the general policy was not to return anyone there, and besides, the only transportation to Iwo was the mail plane. We were determined to give it a try, though, so they let us have a jeep to go on to Advance Headquarters. When we arrived at the Advance Headquarters, we weren't quite sure which way we should tackle the problem of getting those orders. Figuring it was a good idea to grab the dilemma by the horns, and since I was the senior officer in the group, I headed for the first office that appeared to be important. I knocked on the door and my heart beat about three times faster when the voice that answered, "Come in" had a familiar ring. When I opened the door, there, big as life behind the desk, was one of my very close friends from officer's school days in Quantico, Virginia. He was in a rather strategic spot in that Headquarters, so after about a half hour of "old home week" discussions, he went to work on helping us get the orders back to the Fourth Division. It took some real pleading on our part and a lot of assistance from my old friend to get those orders. When we received the orders, they read, "report to the Fourth Marine Division wherever it may be," and we were told that we would have to make whatever arrangements we could at the airfield to get on a plane going to Iwo, and that it wouldn't be easy.

The four of us went to the airfield and checked in at Operations. We were told, "Sorry, nothing but mail and blood plasma going to Iwo right now. You'll have to wait a day or two, and you'll probably go one at a time." As we were leaving the operations office, two pilots walked in to file a flight plan from Guam to Iwo. Now, at last, it was somebody else's turn to have old home week. The pilot of the plane about to leave for Iwo was an old high school buddy of the other Marine captain with me! As you might have already guessed, within an hour the four of us were on that plane headed for Iwo, stretched out on top of the bags of mail and the cartons of blood plasma.

We arrived at Iwo late in the afternoon and within a short time, the four of us were back with our respective units. I have some sad memories on this part of the experience because, of the four of us, one was killed that first night back, another was seriously wounded and evacuated again two days later, and the other two of us were wounded again, though not seriously enough to require evacuation. Every bad situation has a pleasant side, however, and I have many pleasant memories about that trip from Iwo Jima to Guam and back. I'll never forget the wonderful feeling I had at those times when I ran into so many "home folks" within such a short time. I realized that a few people with ties to a small school (3500) or from a small town (21,000), meeting aboard ship and on an island thousands of miles away, were positive proof of that old, shop-worn expression, "Boy, it sure is a small world!" Now, any time I hear anybody make that statement, I automatically say to myself, "Amen!"

My General Officer Assignments

Brigadier General

I served eleven years on active duty as a General Officer, starting with my promotion to Brigadier General in 1968 until my retirement as a Lieutenant General in 1979. As a Brigadier General, my first assignment was at HQMC as Director, Management Analysis Group, reporting directly to the Chief of Staff. I relieved Brigadier General Oscar Peatross in that position.

Taking a hard look at what the Group was doing, and looking at the plan for the future, I was not comfortable with what I saw. As I studied the HQMC organization, one fact jumped out at me. The Marine Corps was just getting into computer-based systems, but there was no central control office to insure that the systems were not overlapping, and were not duplicating demands for input data and thereby burdening the units which were providing the basic reports to the different systems.

I discussed my concerns with LtGen Van Ryzin, the Chief of Staff, and told him I wanted to change the basic mission of the Management Analysis Group so that it would be the coordinator and central control office in HQMC, directly under him as Chief of Staff, for development and implementation of computer-based systems.

He liked the idea and said, "Let's go talk with the Commandant. These computer-based systems are dear to his heart."

I said, "General, I am not ready to present this idea to the Commandant. I just wanted to kick around the concept with you, and when I have a well developed plan, we can present it to the Commandant."

He said, "I like the idea, and I know he will like it, so let's tell him what you plan to do." With that, we went into the Commandant's Office, where the three of us sat around a table and discussed my basic concept of central control of our developing computer-based systems.

I said, "General Chapman, I am not ready to present a fully developed plan to you, but when I discussed my basic concept of centralizing the development and coordination of our computer-based systems with General Van Ryzin, he thought you should know what I believe we need to do. I would expect to get some resistance from the Supply Department and from the Personnel Department because they each have a system underway. But I believe that they can be convinced of the value of coordination as these systems grow and others are added."

General Chapman responded, "Why didn't I think of that? You develop a plan, and at the right time, I will tell the General Officers and others what I have asked you to do, and that may take away some of the resistance. Just hold your plan closely in your Group until we are ready to take the next step."

I prepared a memo for the Chief of Staff, recommending changing the name of the Management Analysis Group to the Systems Support Group, but did not submit it until the Commandant informed the staff about what he had directed me to do.

Director, Marine Corps Development Center

What a joy it was to be told by the Commandant that he was sending me to Quantico to take command of the Development Center. As recounted earlier, in 1950, I was one of three Officers – along with Brigadier General Gerald C. Thomas and Colonel Henry Reid Paige – to establish the Development Center. Now, eighteen years later and as a General Officer to be returning as the Director and on the same organizational level as the Director, Marine Corps Educational Center

(Colonel Louis Wilson) and Commanding General, Marine Corps Base, Quantico, Virginia (Brigadier General Charles Mize), was more than I had dared hoped for. I was told that I would live in Quarters just behind Waller Hall (the historic old building that had become the Base Officers Club), across the circle referred to around the Base as Cocktail Circle, from Colonel Lou Wilson. Once again, I was doing something that I never thought I would do – but I could not have been happier about it.

At the time of my starting my Development Center tour, the Commanding General, Marine Corps Development and Education Command was Lieutenant General Louis Fields, followed by Lieutenant General Ray Davis, followed by Lieutenant General Gay Thrash. I could not have had three better bosses than those three. Living just across Cocktail Circle from Lou Wilson we had a nice social and working relationship, frequently sharing an after-work drink before dinner in their quarters or ours. Martha and Jane had shared time before that when Jane was pregnant with Janet and Martha was pregnant with Brian.

During my time with the Development Center, we wrote the first manual on employment of the AV-8 (Harrier) aircraft, made significant strides in the development of the high-speed air cushion vehicle, and put a lot of emphasis on development of night goggles for the grunts and night vision equipment for helicopters.

I inherited the World's Greatest Secretary, Sylvia Palmer, who was invaluable to me in the front office. She was a very attractive young woman, married, and had a son. She wore the short skirts in vogue at that time, and most Marines who came to my office on business came early so they could look at and talk with Sylvia. She was truly letter perfect in her secretarial duties, took shorthand as fast as I could talk, and brought in finished work that rarely needed any correction. She knew how to receive visitors with a smile and pleasant conversation. She had been in that front office position for several years before I arrived, so she knew a lot of background on matters that I needed to know as the new Director of the Center. I was very fortunate to have her support during my tour as Director of the Development Center.

I made it a point to get away from the Center to visit our defense contractors fairly often, and when General Thrash took over MCDEC, he made a number of those trips with me. Martha and I became very close friends of Gay and Virginia Thrash. After Virginia passed away, Gay married a lovely Marine widow (Woo).

While serving at the Development Center, I was selected for and promoted to the rank of Major General in a brief ceremony in Harry Lee Hall (which had become the Base Officer's Club and BOQ). Within a few days I was called by the Commandant, General Cushman, and told that I would be going to Japan to be the Chief of Staff, U.S. Forces, Japan but it would be a couple of months before I would head for Japan.

The Assistant Commandant called me to say that I could take along an aide (and his family) to Japan and could also take along a steward and his family. From the Development Center troops to which I first looked as the source of an aide, I chose Captain Peter Robertson. After an interview with him, I told him to talk it over with his wife, Suzie, and if they both were willing, I would offer him that assignment. They both accepted with enthusiasm.

Sergeant Henry was already serving as a steward in my Base Quarters, so I offered him and his wife the opportunity to go to Japan. They also accepted with enthusiasm.

They turned out to be good choices. Peter Robinson was very efficient as an Aide and got along wonderfully with the Japanese. Sergeant Henry and his wife had some rough moments in their marriage while in Japan but nothing which I didn't contain in the Marine Corps family. My Quarters in Japan included a Japanese maid (Yoshi) and a Japanese driver (Suwa), whose service and support could not have been better. Did I need all that staff and support? Yes, my job as Chief of Staff required a lot of social entertaining for the Japanese and the NATO Officers (I was Chairman, United Nations Board in Japan), both in my Quarters and out in restaurants and on golf courses, so I needed all that help and sometimes had to get extra assistance.

Major General, Chief of Staff, U.S. Forces, Japan

The billet of Chief of Staff, U.S. Forces, Japan had been the sole province of the U.S. Army, but the Commandant argued that the Marine Corps had the preponderance of forces in the Far East so a Marine should be in that Chief of Staff job. He won, and I became the first Marine to occupy that billet; it has remained in Marine hands since that time.

Over my three years there, I had two fine Officers as my Chief of Staff, one a Navy Captain and the other an Army Colonel. I had a fine staff overall and had only one officer (Army) who had a short tour because he had a son whom he could not control, so the Army called him home rather than risk some untoward incident with the Japanese.

During my tour as Chief of Staff, I worked very closely with three U.S. Ambassadors and developed a close relationship all three of them. My official and personal relationships with them and their wives deserve a long and separate chapter in my life's story.

I had two duties which were of special interest. I was the U.S. Chairman of the Joint Committee, a group of U.S. and Japanese military and civilian (Embassy) personnel, and it was our job to address Status of Forces Agreement problems, military base issues, and other matters involving the U.S.- Japan relationship.

The Japanese Chairman had recently returned from the Japanese Embassy in Washington, DC, spoke flawless English, and was a real joy to work with. He was later Ambassador to Australia and then to the United States. Ambassador Okawara remains a good friend after all these years. He has retired from government service but serves in a "think tank" group which provides advice to the Japanese Government. At the time of my departure from the Hughes office in Tokyo, he spoke at my departure party and lavished great praise on me for my work in Japan as a military man and as a U.S. businessman.

My other duty was as Chairman, United Nations Board in Japan. There were about a dozen NATO nations with military representatives in

Japan, and we met from time to time but had very little real business to attend to. My boss in these NATO matters was General Richard Stillwell, U.S. Army, physically located in Seoul, double-hatted as Commander, U.S. Forces, Korea and Commander, NATO Forces, Far East.

I made a trip to Seoul every few months to call on him and to report on NATO matters in Japan. I was always treated royally on those visits, and when my Japan assignment was terminated, General Stillwell wrote a special letter to the Commandant commending me for my fine work as Chairman, United Nations Board in Japan, stating that I was clearly ready for assignments "of greater responsibilities," and recommending my promotion.

One of the smartest moves I made as the Chief of Staff was related to the American business community in Japan. I wanted the Tokyo/Kanto Plain area American business community to know what U.S. Forces in Japan were doing and wanted them to accept the U.S. Forces as a part of the American expatriate community.

I invited the American Chamber of Commerce in Japan (ACCJ) to my Headquarters at Yokota for a briefing and a tour of the base, to include lunch in a troop mess hall. They accepted and sent two large busloads of ACCJ members out to the base. I personally briefed then about our mission, our force deployments including Okinawa, answered their questions, and went with them as they toured the base, to include the 5th Air Force flight line.

This had never happened to the ACCJ before, and they were extremely appreciative for the program and very pleased that I personally did the briefings and stayed with them for the entire program.

After my Marine Corps retirement, when I returned to Japan in a civilian businessman role, I had lots of new friends in the ACCJ who offered their help as I settled into the expatriate community. Beyond that, several of the Japanese members of the Joint Committee had advanced in their respective Ministries, and a couple of them had become Ambassadors. Each of them contacted me to offer their help to me as I settled in as a civilian businessman. A number of Self Defense Force

Officers had advanced to senior positions, and I was able to capitalize on the friendships I had made in my military position.

My military assignment in Japan was a happy one and very successful. I stayed in that position for three years because the Ambassador and CINCPAC (Admiral Gayler) did not want me to leave. I left the position after three years with the help of Admiral Gayler when he learned that General Lou Wilson had been nominated for Commandant and that he had asked me to accept the three-star position as Marine Corps Operations Deputy to the Joint Chiefs of Staff. That was a logical assignment for me because of my joint service in Europe and in Japan, and I had cultivated a good reputation with several Members of the Joint Chiefs principals and the Joint Staff.

General Wilson told me that after two years in the OPDEP job, he wanted me to become Chief of Staff at HQMC. What more could a Major General ask, particularly when I did not have much confidence that there would be a three-star position available for me under the General Cushman regime?

General Wilson told me that he was bringing in Major General Les Brown to be the Chief of Staff and Major General Bob Barrow as head of the Manpower Department. I was senior to both of those officers through all my years of service, but both of them became senior to me as Lieutenant Generals because they were there in mid-Summer when General Wilson took office and I did not report for duty until 1 September. Under the system, your date of rank takes effect on the day you move into the job which requires a Lieutenant General. I don't believe that seniority had any real impact on the choice between Bob Barrow and me for the Commandant's position four years later.

Want to know what I did in my job as Chief of Staff, U.S. Forces, Japan? Going through my Marine Corps records, I found a document written to support the Distinguished Service Medal award for my service, and I was fascinated to read it. In my view, the authors of that document really did a lot of staff research to put that document together. There are descriptions of programs that only certain members of my

USFJ Staff would have known about, some matters which were clearly known to the 5th Air Force, and some matters which were known in most detail by the U.S. Embassy Staff. I was impressed when I read it.

Marine Corps Operations Deputy to the Joint Chiefs of Staff

I arrived at HQMC on 6 August 1975 and began reading about the duties and responsibilities of the OPDEP. I was promoted to the rank of Lieutenant General on 1 September with the retirement of LtGen Herb Beckington, who had used a Congressional connection (Hubert Humphrey) to get General Wilson to let him stay until that date. In the long run, it didn't really make any difference, but I didn't like it at the time.

In any event, I went about my new duties with great enthusiasm because I was right at home with so many folks over in the JCS arena. Martha and I moved into Quarters #4 at Marine Barracks, 8th and I Streets, SE and began to enjoy being there with all those young Marines, the Marine Corps Band, and the Commandant's Own Drum and Bugle Corps. We lived next door to Center House, the Officer's Club for the Barracks Officers, and we had many happy hours with those sharp young Marine Officers who performed in the parades and all the military events that happened in Washington. It was a great four years for us, particularly while our son Steve was stationed there and had his family in nearby Woodbridge, Virginia. I was tremendously fortunate to work closely with such successful and important people.

Chief of Staff, Headquarters, US Marine Corps

What an assignment to have as my final job in the Marine Corps! The Commandant told me one afternoon as we were returning from a JCS meeting that tomorrow he would tell Les Brown that he was being transferred to Hawaii to be CG, FMF, Pac and I would become Chief of Staff. He would bring in Dolph Shwenk to relieve me as the JCS OpDep.

Les Brown and I had been friends since about 1950 or so. We sat together and discussed the timing of the turnover of the Chief's Office. We kept it very simple, and with a handshake, I moved into the Chief's chair and Les went on leave before heading to Hawaii. When the time came for Les to retire, the Commandant sent me out there to the Change of Command ceremony as his Representative.

Within a few days of taking the Chief's chair, I gathered all General Officers in a conference room of the Headquarters to give them a few statements about how I planned to operate as the Chief of Staff. My guidance went along these lines:

"All of us Generals at the Headquarters are here to support the Commandant in all internal and external matters related to the Marine Corps. Beyond that, my primary responsibility is to coordinate all of your staff efforts, and let me be clear about one thing: I am a nut about staff coordination. When a paper comes to me, I will expect that it has been fully coordinated with every staff section that will be affected by it. The Commandant is the final decision maker. Our job is to give him the facts related to the problems which face him and give him our best judgment as to what his decisions should be.

"My first rule is that nothing goes to the Commandant without going through me. I may not agree with your point of view, but I will never stop you from presenting your views directly to the Commandant. Within your areas of responsibility, I urge you to make decisions contrary to policy when you believe it is right to do so, but be sure you blind copy me so I can advise the Commandant. If you make a mistake, we will work our way around it, and I promise to be on your side if I am content that your intentions were well meaning.

"My door is always open to each of you Generals. If my outer office folks say I am busy, you can still walk in if you believe you have an urgent need to talk with me. Selection Boards chose you because they were confident that you could handle positions of great responsibility, and you are here because the Commandant has confidence in you, and so do I. Working together, I have high confidence that we are going to help an outstanding Commandant do even better. I know all of you join with me in that challenge."

One day I received a phone call from Ambassador Shirley Temple Black, our U.S. Ambassador to Switzerland. (That is Shirley Temple, child star of movie fame, whose videos of her several movies are still big sellers.) She was calling about a Marine in her Embassy who she said was doing a fine job but was scheduled to be transferred to Camp Lejeune to an infantry battalion. Shea asked if I could please let him stay for another year. I told her that one of my jobs was to insure that Marine Corps needs come first; the individual Marine's career interests come second.

I said that I would take a look at his record and let her know as soon as feasible. She said she could not ask more than that, and we terminated the call. After looking at his record, I decided he would enhance his Marine Corps career (he was on his second reenlistment) by getting back with our Operating Forces and sent a message to the Detachment Commander at our Embassy directing him to inform Ambassador Black of my decision. I heard nothing further from the Ambassador.

Almost every week I received a call from a Congressman or one of his Staff members inquiring about the welfare or troubling situation of a Marine, usually as a follow-up to a letter from the Marine's mother saying her son was not getting enough to eat or was not being promoted as he had been promised. Most of those inquiries were handled routinely, and the bulk of them turned out to be complaints of a homesick young Marine who had not adapted well to the Marine Corps system. In one case, a mother had complained that her son was dissatisfied with his food and was not getting enough to eat. I had that Marine's chow line choices monitored for one week and found that, for each meal, he chose only the meat entrée and nothing else, ignoring all vegetables and deserts and other food choices. After a lot of useless effort, the case was resolved without difficulty.

When the Assistant Commandant (Sam Jaskilka) retired, Bob Barrow was given that position. From my point of view, that meant he would succeed Lou Wilson as Commandant. Bob had an outstanding record, gained a lot of publicity when he led his Regiment into Laos under the top leadership of General Ray Davis, and had lots of the right friends in Congress.

I told General Wilson that, in my view, I was at the end of my trail, and that I was ready to retire when he thought the timing was right. He insisted that I not retire, saying that I was highly competitive to be his successor and that in his view, Bob and I were the two top candidates for his job.

I said that I could not find any justification for going around Bob, already a four-star General, to get to me. There were several newspaper articles, including one from the San Diego newspaper, saying that Bob Barrow and I were the top contenders, but that was only speculation. Further, I knew that, when the time came for a new Commandant, the Secretary of the Navy and the Secretary of Defense looked at all the Lieutenant Generals and sometimes chose someone else further down the lineal list. (General Shoup was a good example.)

While I was on a three-day speaking tour in the southeast, supporting our recruiters, President Jimmy Carter called Bob to the White House and informed him of his appointment. I returned late that evening, and the next morning as soon as he arrived, General Wilson called me in to tell me that the President had chosen Bob.

I told the Commandant that I was not at all surprised, and that I would request retirement at the soonest possible date so Bob could start moving his team into place. I then went to Bob Barrow's office, offered him my congratulations, and told him that that I would request immediate retirement so he could start to move in his new team.

As I said in another place, there are no losers when everybody wins. Bob went on to be a fine Commandant, and I went on to a fine job in the civilian corporate world which put my life in a new direction. The Marine Corps won, Bob Barrow won, and I won. God works in mysterious ways, but somehow he finds a solution that puts all those involved in positions that are best for them in the long term.

Reversion to the Snowden Clan

Growing up in Charlottesville was not particularly exciting, but it was a quiet, safe, and friendly place where families knew a lot about each other or at least knew something about them. Even in the friendliest of places, children, particularly in their early teens, can be mean and ugly to one another, and the name of Snoddy gave them the opportunity to be mean when they wanted to be.

In some cases, they were not really trying to be mean, but used variations of the name to tease me. In other cases, boys were trying to "bring me down a peg" because they were jealous of my popularity with the girls and that I was an open favorite of many of the teachers.

I sang at a number of school assemblies, had the male lead in every musical play for three years, and held a number of elected positions (President of the Boys Glee Club and President of the HiY Club, both for Lane High School and for the Central District of Virginia, and several others). I sincerely believe that petty jealousy was the root of much of the ugly teasing.

The Snoddy family has roots back to the early 1700s and, in the main on my father's side, settled in central Virginia in Fluvanna and Buckingham counties, later migrating the thirty-mile distance to Charlottesville. My paternal grandfather, Marion Ivan Snoddy, had owned and operated a general store right alongside one of the popular roads in Fluvanna County.

After the family relocated to the big city, he operated a small grocery store on 4th Street, less than a block away from Main Street. I cannot document it, but I recall the store was simply the "4th Street Market." With my grandfather, my father and two uncles meeting the public in a number of places, the family name was fairly well known around the town. Away from Charlottesville, however, it was an unusual family name.

As I increasingly was thrown before public audiences during my high school years, the more I noticed the snickers and comments that rippled through the audiences when I was introduced. My first real encounter came when I was invited to do a weekly radio show on Radio Station WCHV in Charlottesville. It was my show as a singer, and I was accompanied by Bus Smith on guitar, Ben Borden on piano, and Harry James on string bass, three truly professional musicians with whom I worked in the several dance bands for which I was the singer.

When we first met to talk about the format for the show, Ed Hayes, one of the station managers and their top announcer, said he would be the announcer for the show. He then said, "We sure as hell can't call it the Larry Snoddy show. What title will we use? Larry, you are going to have to adopt a show name. What name do you want?"

Worried about embarrassing my family members, I said, "Ed, I am not ready to do that."

Ed said, "Come on, all the Hollywood stars use stage names, you can do it too."

I said, "No, I won't do that."

Ed said, "OK. Let's consider our alternatives."

After lots of discussion, we settled on "Larry Presents Bus, Ben, and Harry." The thirty-minute weekly show went on for five months, and we stopped only because Bus Smith and his Orchestra had too many engagements and Bus could no longer spare the time for my show. (Incidentally, I was the male vocalist for the Bus Smith Orchestra for three years, but I also sang with the Hartwell Clark Orchestra and the Bruce Hangar Orchestra when Bus had open dates.)

Why do I remember the precise words said about the plans for my show? Because it was my first encounter in which a public program refused to use my family name. That experience stuck with me.

Skipping over some incidents of lesser importance, I jump to 1954 when I came home from the Korean War and was assigned as Officer in Charge, Marine Corps Recruiting Station, New York City. About that time, a very popular book was published: *Battle Cry,* by Leon Uris, and it immediately was made into a movie. It was about Marines and had many incidents of Marines fighting among themselves in their barracks. The Marine Corps Public Information Office, located directly above my office at 346 Broadway in lower Manhattan, decided we needed to do something to counter all the bad publicity for the Marine Corps associated with *Battle Cry.* That office arranged with a theater owner in Jersey City to select a pretty girl as Miss Battle Cry, and I would crown her on the theater stage just before the movie began.

I wore my blue uniform. The theater was full. The local Master of Ceremonies pumped up the audience with funny stories and jokes about Marines, and then had Miss Battle Cry sit in a high-back red velvet chair. Then he said, "Miss Battle Cry will now be presented her crown by the Officer in Charge of the New York Recruiting Station, Major Lawrence Snoddy."

Most of the theater audience had not heard that family name before, and the usual sniggles and comments went throughout the theater. The theater manager later told me he was "sorry about that," but he didn't know what to do about it.

This was another experience that stuck in my memory craw, but like the theater manager, I really didn't know what to do about it.

I decided to do two things: Look at other names that came from the same area in Wales (Northern England), and talk with my mother about the matter. What she had to say both surprised me and stopped me in my tracks (at least temporarily).

I learned that the Snoddy name had at least two other spellings back in Wales, Snowday and Snowdon. I also learned that the region in Wales included Mount Snowden, which was also referred to as Mount Snowdon. To keep the tie to the area which seemed to be the origin of the family, I chose Snowden.

At home one weekend, I took mother aside and gave her all my thoughts on the matter. Her surprising response went essentially as follows:

a.   I have always loved going to the movies and I particularly loved the musical movies.

b.   As I watched those musical movies and listened to the male singers, it was my dream that some day, I would see you singing in a movie. I knew that you had the looks, the voice and the talent to do that.

c.   I also knew that if you were to go into the movies, you would have to adopt a stage name and I then asked myself, "How will anyone know he is my son if he changes his name?"

d.   That is the only question I have for you now. How will anyone know you are my son if you change your name? The enormous pride I have in you for what you have done, for becoming a General in the Marine Corps, for the wonderful reputation you have gained. All these things make me take a very jealous position on this matter. I want you to do what you believe is best for your future, and if you decide to make the change, I will find a way to live with it.

My answer took only an instant. I said, "I have made no decision at this time. I just wanted to discuss the matter with you. I will tell you now that it is a dead issue for now, and you will not have to worry about it during your life time."

Many years later, I was a Brigadier General, Director of the Marine Corps Development Center, when I received word that I would be going to Japan as Chief of Staff, U.S. Forces, Japan and would be promoted to Major General before departing Quantico.

As I thought about going to Japan, I thought that it might be the right time to get on with the reversion to the Snowden name, which I had set aside until after my mother's death. I figured that the assignment to Japan would give me the chance for a new start with a new name – time for that change to become known throughout the Marine Corps before I returned to duty in the Marine Corps from the joint assignment.

I contacted the Base Legal Officer and asked for his advice. He said it was a simple process that required court approval, but he could take care of the whole thing and that I would not have to appear in court.

So, with that knowledge in hand, I sat down with Martha and developed my plan of action, called Steve and Brian to discuss it with them, and assured them they were not bound by my action in the matter. They could choose whether to follow suit and when to take action if they decided to make the change. (Both of them did make the change independently from my action.)

I called on the Assistant Commandant, LtGen E. O. Anderson, and the Commandant, General Robert Cushman, and informed them of my plans. I said to General Cushman that I wanted his permission.

His response was, "You don't need my permission. That is your personal business, and I completely support what you plan to do."

The name change having been decided on, I called the Base Legal Officer and asked him to proceed with the court papers. It was only a matter of weeks before I had court approval.

I had to decide on how I would make the announcement on Base about the name change. Base Maintenance changed the nameplate on the front door of our Quarters and the name sign which was in the front yard for easy visibility from the street. I was scheduled to speak to the Junior School class about the concept and the projects ongoing in the Development Center. I decided that would be a good captive audience, and the timing was just right.

When I was being introduced, I had a large screen chart that included the crest of the Development Center and across the top of the chart was, "Director, Marine Corps Development Center, Brigadier General Lawrence F. Snoddy." That screen stayed on until I had completed the first couple of paragraphs of my remarks. At that point, the same crest screen came on, but this time across the top of the chart it read, "Director, Marine Corps Development Center, Brigadier General Lawrence F. Snowden."

There was a collective gasp from the audience, and without waiting for a question, I said, "You will note that over the course of my visit with you, I have changed my identity. After considerable research, I have returned to my original family name with roots back to Wales, in Northern England. I found several different spellings of the original family name, but chose this one, which was used when the family settled in Virginia in the 1700s. It may take some time for the word to get around, but the change takes place today, and I wanted you to be the first to know. Semper Fidelis."

That brought smiles and a hearty round of applause.

Later that same day, the newspaper published in Woodbridge, Virginia, came out with a full-page spread about the name change, complete with several pictures of me and activities of the Development Center. The Base Information Officer made a release after the Legal Officer reported the change at the Base Commander's staff meeting. Since it was all positive, I really had nothing to complain about.

Another, but much smaller version was run in the Stars and Stripes Newspaper, a military newspaper with a large circulation among the military forces around the world, but of particular interest in Japan because the paper had learned that I was going to become the next Chief of Staff, U.S. Forces, Japan. So much for getting off to a new identity.

And so the new Snowden Clan came into being, and as I look back these many years later, I know I did the right thing. Sometimes, even now, an old friend will refer to me by the old family name and then immediately offer some word of apology. I quickly say, "No problem. No apology is needed. That simply shows you are a friend of long standing."

U.S.-Japan Attitude Change:

Slow But Inevitable

Q: General, as a World War II veteran you had to have an anti-Japanese attitude about the Japanese. Obviously, as I know about your work with the Japanese today, somewhere along the line you must have had a complete change of attitude. Can you explain that?

Snowden: That is a question I have been asked before, so I have a ready answer. While fighting in Korea about six months prior to the Armistice Agreement, I was ordered to Kyoto, Japan, for a logistic conference which included the other US Forces, along with a number of Japanese agencies which were involved with the trans-shipments of arms and armaments from Japanese ports to Korean ports in support of US Forces and their Allies. During that three-day conference, I worked closely with other US Forces and the Japanese conferees. I sat with them at the conference table, dined with them, socialized with them, and discovered that the folks I used to call enemy were no longer enemies but were cooperating as friends working together for a common cause. I found them to be extremely courteous, friendly, and great supporters of our Korean War efforts. Returning to Korea and eventually back home, I found myself with a new, completely different attitude about Japan and its people. That new concept and mind-set became important when, in 1972, I was promoted to Major General and assigned to Japan as Chief of Staff, US Forces, Japan---a billet which I occupied for three years.

In addition to the Chief of Staff billet, I was the US Chairman of the Joint Committee which handled the day-to-day problems of military base issues and other matters related to the Mutual Security Agreement between Japan and the US. The Japan Chairman of the Joint Committee was Yoshio Okawara, later Japan's Ambassador to the United States. I still give great credit to Ambassador Okawara for teaching me so much about the culture of Japan and for invaluable information about how the Japanese government went about its day-to-day business. All that became very important when I retired from the Marine Corps and returned to Japan as an international businessman based in Tokyo but responsible for programs in Japan, Korea and Taiwan.

Within two years of returning to Japan as an international businessman, I was elected President of the American Chamber of Commerce in Japan (ACCJ), and in that capacity, I worked closely with a number of Japanese government agencies on US-Japan trade problems, mostly related to automobiles and electronic programs along with issues of restrictions on foreign lawyers practicing in Japan. The senior government officials with whom I had been working as Chief of Staff, US Forces, Japan proved to be very helpful to me in my civilian position. The Japanese do not forget their friends.

Q: It is my understanding that you also had a NATO responsibility. What was that?

Snowden: I was Chairman of the NATO Board in Japan and in that capacity I reported to the Commander, NATO Forces, Far East , Headquartered in Korea. I made quarterly trip to Seoul to report to him. The NATO Board members in Tokyo were mostly Military Attaches on Embassy Staffs of NATO Members with presence in Tokyo. The provided me with another, but different, set of valuable contacts in Japan.

Q: What about your social contacts in Japan? Were you and your wife active in the social world?

Snowden: That requires a long answer but since you asked, here it is. Thanks to some good Japanese friends, I was invited to join the exclusive Tokyo Club. It was a club for gentlemen only. Ladies were invited in only once a year. Membership included members of the Royal Family, former prime ministers, senior members of the Diet (Japanese Congress), and some of the industrial giants who brought prosperity to Japan after WWII.

I was present when the Crown Prince (now Emperor) and his Princess arrived at the Tokyo Club for his annual visit circa 1987. I was introduced and had the time to say a brief hello, but had no other contact with either of them. They were both most impressive and pleasant.

I was admitted to the Tokyo Tennis Club where many members from the foreign diplomatic community played tennis and socialized. Among those, I met and had lunch with the Russian Ambassador which gained me invitations to the Russian Embassy for several special events.

I was a Member, and later a Board Member, of the Tokyo American Club which was a "must-join" organization for American businessmen and major Japanese corporations, a central location where business and social activities provided useful interface for companies doing business in Japan. The Club provided a busy schedule of social events which did a lot to facilitate business in the office after friendships were established socially.

As President of the American Chamber of Commerce in Japan, I had an extremely busy schedule briefing executives of American corporations who were interested in doing business in Japan and who sought help from Chamber Members who had already achieved success in Japan. Because of my position as President of the Chamber, I was invited to a number of programs by Keidanren and often asked to present views of the Chamber on trade issues. (Keidanren is roughly comparable to the United States Chamber of Commerce located in Washington, DC.) I was the first foreigner in ten years to address a committee of Diet Members on trade issues. Scheduled for one hour, the session lasted for three hours and I received several letters from those committee members for my presentation and for my willingness to handle so many questions in the extended meeting.

Tokyo Baptist Church. Martha and I lived in the Ichigaya section of Tokyo, very near to the Shinjuku section which was almost as popular as downtown and the Ginza. We visited several English-speaking

churches near our neighborhood and after several months we found the
Tokyo Baptist Church, about twenty minutes drive in the opposite
direction from my office. We knew we had the right church because it
had Southern Baptist minister with a real Texas drawl, a small choir, and
a real organ. I joined the choir right away and right way became the
primary soloist. Every Sunday after the church service, there was a full
breakfast in the lower-level conference room, and Martha quickly earned
the title of "the Biscuit Lady" because she could turn out batches of
biscuits as fast as the folks could eat them, and the Japanese members
loved those freshly baked, hot biscuits. We had a new set of contacts, to
include a group of missionaries who sought to convert Japanese families
to Christianity. Using a portable karaoke machine, I often accompanied
the missionaries to Japanese homes and sang several hymns to get the
home service started — a personally rewarding experience.

You asked if we mixed in socially in Tokyo. I think we did and
often extended our social exchanges to Yokohama and Yokosuka. I think
we sometimes overdid it, but I never regretted a moment of it. It certainly
was part of why we enjoyed Japan so much.

*Q: That pretty much answers my basic questions. Since I am focusing on how
US businessmen find success in the difficult Japanese market, is there any
comment you would care to add related to your own success in Japan?*

Snowden: I had the good fortune to work closely with three US
ambassadors to Japan: Robert Ingersoll, James Hodgson, and Mike
Mansfield. My relationship with each of them was slightly different, but
I was privileged in each case to have a personal relationship with them
and their wives which went beyond simply an official relationship.

Ambassador Ingersoll: Shortly after my arrival as Chief of Staff,
US Forces, Japan, I was invited to join with Ambassador Ingersoll at a
dinner given in his honor by the Japanese Minister of Defense. It was a
typical Japanese men's dinner, complete with a geisha companion seated
next to each guest to help him with his food, keep him supplied with
cigarettes, and just be pleasant. The custom in Japan is that after dinner,
everyone will do something to entertain the other dinner companions.

The Ambassador was an excellent harmonica player and usually carried three harmonicas in his pockets. He had a large one (10" or so), a medium size (6" or so) and a small one of about 4", and he was master of them all. First up was the Defense Minister who sang an old WWII fighting song. Then the Ambassador played a mix of US and Japanese songs. Next, a staff member of the Foreign Office recited an old Japanese poem. Then it was my turn, so I sang, "On the Street Where You Live" (from *My Fair Lady*). Since I was the only real singer in the group, it was a big hit and helped me with a lot of good contacts later. That night set the precedent, and the Ambassador and I teamed up for several such dinners after that. With that kind of good start, I had a good relationship with the Ambassador, and on a number of occasions, Martha and I were invited to Embassy functions, to include dinners when Ingersoll family members were in town.

Ambassador Hodgson: Martha and I were invited to join with the Ambassador and his wife as guests of the Commander, Maritime Self-Defense Force for the Black Ship Festival, a festival remembering the arrival in Japan of Commodore Perry, demanding that Japan open up the country to foreign trade. We were aboard a small Japanese ship when a storm moved in, and it was decided that the Ambassador's party would transfer to a US destroyer for return to Tokyo. The ships were lined up side by side and a small gangplank was put down for us to cross over. When Mrs. Hodgson had two steps onto the plank, a large wave hit the ships and Mrs. Hodgson was thrown off balance but caught by several of us standing at each end of the plank. A major disaster was avoided, but it put the fear of possible disaster into all of us. We returned to Tokyo without further problem but with a memorable experience. That incident brought us closer together as friends.

Ambassador Mansfield: I had met him when he was President of the Senate and had a start on friendship because of his time in the Marine Corps. He had been stationed in the Philippines as a Corporal and gave total credit to the Marine Corps for that assignment which caused him to take a deep interest in Asia and its potential problems. He wore the Marine Tie Bar on his tie every day. When I arrived in Japan as a civilian businessman, he welcomed me like an old friend and gave me a special number to call if I wanted to see him, with no need to go through the Embassy switchboard or his secretary. I became instant friends with the Marine Detachment, which provided internal security for the Embassy. Martha and I were frequent visitors to Ambassador's residence. At several Embassy social functions, he asked us to stand at the front entrance of the residence to say good night to the guests on his behalf. On my departure from Japan, he wrote (by hand) a very flattering letter commending me for my assistance to him and for my good work in strengthening the Japan–US relationship. That letter is one of my greatest treasures.

In sum, I believe that I achieved a certain level of success in my military and my civilian assignments, but I know that a lot of credit must go to American friends and to my Japanese friends who always lent a hand when I needed one.

The Reunion of Honor

The first time a group of survivors returned to Iwo Jima was in 1985. Two years earlier, a group centered in the Camp Pendleton/San Diego area decided they would like to go there to celebrate the 40th anniversary of that battle. One member of the group was a travel agent with an office in San Diego, so he set up the air travel arrangements. They appealed to the Commanding General, Fleet Marine Forces, Pacific, based in Honolulu, to help get them there from Tokyo.

When the group reached Honolulu, Lieutenant General Charlie Cooper met them and told them that he had arranged for the air force to fly them from Yokota Air Base in Japan to Iwo Jima. One of the survivors asked Charlie whether they would have to pay extra for that flight. Charlie gave them an answer they would long remember. He said, "We didn't charge you for the first time you went, and we won't charge you this time." The Air Force flew us all down there in C-130s.

I had nothing to do with the arrangements for that trip. I was living and working in Tokyo at that time, so I joined the group at Yokota Air Base for the Iwo Jima visit. As we stood around on the island talking, several suggested it would be great if we could make the trip again on the 50th anniversary of the battle. We laughed and said, "But how many of us will still be here to make the trip ten years from now?'

The 1985 visit was not advertised as a joint reunion, though it turned out to be joint because of the efforts of a Buddhist priest named Tunezo Wachi. He was known to many in the 4th Marine Division Association because he had attended several of their association reunions and was known as "the Reverend." He had a unique history. He was graduated from the Japanese Naval Academy (Eta Jima) in 1923, served with a cavalry regiment, was an intelligence officer and a spy at the Japanese Embassy in Mexico City, and later commanded the Japanese garrison on Iwo Jima during most of 1944. At some point which I cannot recall, he was returned to Japan before the battle in 1945 and commanded a squadron of "suicide boats" which were actually manned torpedoes developed to be used against our troop ships when we invaded Japan. He and his daughter, Rosa Ogawa, a travel agent who spoke excellent English, helped set up the 1985 trip to Iwo Jima and are credited with establishing the Japan Iwo Jima Association. To his credit, Wachi spent most of his post-war life serving the souls of those Japanese men who lost their lives on Iwo Jima. He was truly a remarkable man.

In early 1994, several of the group called me and asked if the trip could be made in 1995 to observe the 50th anniversary. I told them I would look into it. By this time Warren Wiedhahn, Colonel, USMC, Retired, had "Military Historical Tours" up and running and being very successful in battlefield tours to Guam, Pelileu, and to the European Theater. I called him and told him of the interest in the Iwo trip in 1995. Together we thought it was worth exploring but, based on my military and civilian experience in Japan, I thought it would be great if some Japanese survivors could join us for a joint memorial service honoring the dead on both sides of the battle.

Warren and I headed for Tokyo to call on Ambassador Walter Mondale and senior members of the Japanese government. I had a number of good contacts in Tokyo, but knew I would need the ambassador's support to convince the Japanese side, particularly at the foreign minister level. No surprise to me, but initial opposition to the joint memorial service idea came from middle-level bureaucrats in the foreign ministry who were sincerely afraid that we Americans would somehow turn the event into a celebration of our victory there. I pledged on my personal integrity that there would be no suggestion of any victory and that our sole purpose for the joint reunion would be to honor the dead on both sides and to pledge on both sides that we would work together as friends and allies to insure that such warfare that existed on

Iwo Jima would never happen again. I am pleased to say that, after twenty years of the "Reunion of Honor, we have never had an untoward incident on the island and the Reunion of Honor has come to be recognized as an "alliance-building" event which strengthens the bilateral relationship between our two nations.

The 1995 Reunion of Honor got the event off to a great start because our special guest and speaker was the widow of LTGEN Kuribayashi who commanded the Japanese forces on Iwo Jima. There is no way we could have done any better than that. She spoke in old classical Japanese and many of the young Japanese present could not understand her. Her words were priceless. She said that once we were enemies and now we are friends and together we must insure that never again will there be war like that which took place on Iwo Jima. Her words have been echoed throughout a number of memorial service speeches since 1995.

Also present was the grandson of LTGEN Kuribayashi, the Honorable Yoshitaka Shindo, member of the House of Representatives in the Japanese *Diet* (their Congress). He has attended every Reunion of Honor since that time and continues to be a strong supporter of the Iwo Jima association of Japan. We have become "embracing friends" over the years.

Also present was Mr. Yasunori Nishi, the son of Baron Nishi, the famous Japanese horseman who won a gold medal in the 1932 Olympics and was killed on Iwo Jima. Mr. Nishi was a Colonel. Happily, we have remembered each other over the years. We too are "embracing friends," and that is important because, in Japan, who you know is more important than what you know.

What about the future of the Reunion of Honor? That question cannot be answered at this time. For the record, however, I need to comment on the Iwo Jima Association of America, the Reunion of Honor, and Military Historical Tours. These are three different entities which are bound together by the Iwo Jima anniversaries.

Major General Fred Haynes deserves full credit for founding the

Combat Veterans of Iwo Jima, which has been renamed the Iwo Jima Associates of America (IJAA). That change was made to recognize that there were many who supported the Iwo Jima battle but did not face any combat. Further, we recognized that we needed to have younger family members involved if the organization was to have a long-term existence, so we needed ways to enlarge our membership. That has worked out well. The IJAA sponsors the anniversary program at Quantico on or about 19 February each year. The program now has the support of the National Museum of the Marine Corps and Headquarters, Marine Corps with the Commandant or the Assistant Commandant participating.

The Joint Reunion of Honor is a separate entity which I founded in 1995. As stated previously, with Warren Wiedhahn along to handle all the logistics questions, I went to Tokyo and sold the joint reunion idea to the Japanese, with the help of Ambassador Mondale. It has grown in popularity and in stature and is now recognized as an important alliance-building event between Japan and the United States. Though the number of living survivors of the Iwo Jima battle is declining rapidly, family members on both sides want the event to continue.

The IJAA and the Reunion of Honor are joined at the hip in our three-way relationship with Military Historical Tours. Essentially, what happens is that I contract with Military Historical Tours to arrange the chartered aircraft required to take us from Guam to Iwo Jima. It is a no-profit added leg to MHT's tour to Guam. Warren and his very able staff provide all the administrative support from, advertising, to hotel accommodations, to working with the several active-duty Marine Corps units which provide our ceremonial support, and local liaison with the Japanese Embassy in Washington. Warren has been invaluable to the Reunion of Honor program, and his staff members have served with distinction since the outset.

The Declining Decade

From a statistical standpoint, it can be expected that God will probably call me home to the Big Marine Corps Base in the Sky sometime in the 2016-2020 timeframe, and I think I will be ready for that. It is not with any sense of pessimism that I label this piece as "The Declining Decade."

It is logical for me to say that the decline started with the loss of Martha in July 2006. Having dealt with death so much in my three wars, Martha's death did not devastate me as would normally be expected after 63 years of marriage. I recognized death when I saw it, and had long ago accepted the idea that death was simply the final step in the life cycle and, no matter who you were, life was going to go on. It was a shock for me, of course, but in hindsight, I know that God was good to her and good to me. He was good to her in that he took her home swiftly and without pain. The doctors who attended her in the emergency room of Capital Regional Hospital told me that her heart just stopped; there was no time for pain. When it is time for my death, I would hope that it happens that way to me.

God was good to me in that he did not leave me with an incapacitated spouse, bedridden and without the mental capacity to know me. I have several friends with spouses who have been bedridden for several years, who they visit every day out of love and loyalty, but without any recognition about them being present. None of them would say that situation is a burden, but we all know otherwise. I am fortunate that it didn't happen to me.

About one year after Martha's death, I was contacted by Beverly

Ewald about going with her to a Tallahassee Symphony Orchestra concert at FSU. She explained that the lady friend who usually went with her was out of town, so she had the extra ticket.

A little background is needed here about Beverly and her second husband, Chuck. They were one of our first family friends soon after our arrival in Tallahassee. I played golf with Chuck in the Tuesday seniors group, and later, Beverly joined the choir that I had joined right after our arrival. So we were together socially at a number of events. When Chuck died, I sang at his funeral, and when Martha died a couple of years later, Beverly was the first one at my door to see what she could do to help. That is the background to the relationship which I developed with Beverly.

I told her that I had wanted to attend a lot of the programs available at FSU but I could not handle the parking problems, so I had kind of given up on those events. She said, "I know how difficult that is, but as a member of the Board for the Symphony, I have a special parking space right across the street from the front entrance to Ruby Diamond Auditorium. Would you reconsider?"

I said, "Beverly, for the cheap price of a parking space, you have just made a special friend. I will be pleased to accept your invitation."

Riding down to the concert and back home, we talked about our mutual interests in musical events and decided that with my driving and her parking space, we would be going to a lot of events together. And that is how it has worked out. We are senior citizen companions who provide a lot of support to each other.

My move from McLaughlin Drive to Westminster Oaks came about in an odd way. I had previously looked at Westminster, but did not see an apartment that was centrally located, and I did not want to get on a waiting list that was uncertain in every way. After my hip surgery and while I was still in the hospital, Brian and Julia asked if I had any interest in moving in to Westminster. I said no and explained why. They said they would like to look at it anyway if I had no objection.

They went to Westminster Oaks for a tour and were shown the apartment that I later moved into. They saw it just as it was being finished refurbishing. The marketing director told them that it would be available, and they would start calling folks on the waiting list. When they came back to the hospital and reported on their visit, I asked what was meant when the marketing director said it was available. I asked Brian to give the lady a call to clarify that statement. She told him that she had already made several calls and had three declines because it was larger than those folks wanted. She concluded by saying, "Tell your father he can have it if he wants it."

I said, "I need to see it, but I will need a wheelchair. Let's see if we can set it up right away."

We came out to see it, and as soon as I entered the apartment, I knew it was meant for me. I said, "Let's sign the papers so I can move in when I am out of the hospital."

And that is how it worked. I believe the marketing director knew that the apartment was a little larger than most folks wanted, and the "buy-in fee" was a little pricey, so I made out. It was the right move for me.

I could not have cleared out my McLaughlin Drive house of twenty-three years and moved into Westminster Oaks without exceptional help from Barbara, Steve, Brian, Julia, and Jeffrey. They all worked tirelessly to get the job done, and there is no way I could reward them for their good work. I just know that I had magnificent family support, and there is no way to adequately reward that.

I expect to remain at Westminster Oaks until my demise – however long that may be.

Yes, There Can Be Hell on Earth

At no time in my earlier years did I believe I would live to be 95 years old, but here we are. Of course I don't know how much longer I will be here, but I want to wrap up the Snowden Story just in case there is a need for another tome about me, a family member or a friend. I am kidding, of course. There is no way I could be talked into undertaking another book.

I started the Snowden Story about two years ago by dropping notes in a file folder about events I wanted to remember to tell my family. My sole purpose (unchanged) was to record for my great, great grandchildren (strictly family) something about my life because they didn't get to see me or know me. As I fumbled for a way to find closure, I found that the period from April 2015 to April 2016 included events which were the lows and the highs of my life and I was just about to ignore them. Makes me wonder if I am more senile than I think I am.

I start with the lows. When I returned to Tallahassee after the March 2015 Joint US-Japan Reunion of Honor on Iwo Jima, I was physically and mentally exhausted. I had pneumonia, a congested heart valve which caused labored breathing, and a deep, rumbling cough along with the other miseries associated with congestive heart disease. The first doctor I saw admitted me immediately to the hospital, with primary concern over the congested heart valve. The heart valve team took an inside look at the valve and said I would need to repair/replace the valve but thought that I was several months away from surgery. As it turned out, less than two months after that prognosis, I was on the surgery table having a total new bovine skin valve replacement. It is working wonderfully and has given me a new life in the heart arena.

Between that time and October, I was hospitalized three more times with pneumonia and other miseries, but there were no instances worthy of reporting. The king daddy of the lows started the day I fell in my Assisted Living apartment and broke my right thigh bone (femur) and really has not ended as I write this in August 2016. It was a Sunday afternoon; I was in my kitchenette standing with my Rollator in hand. Son Brian was sitting on the sofa in my living room. For reasons which I do not remember, I started out for my bedroom and after I rounded the corner of kitchen counter, I felt myself leaning to the right and I said, "I am going down, Brian, I'm going down." And with that, down I went on my right side. I knew immediately that this fall was different. Something was different, something was broken, and the pain was beyond severe. I did not know whether it was the replaced hip or something else, but the pain was beyond dreadful. I was screaming in pain as I said, "Call 911." But someone had already done that, and the EMS team responded within minutes.

As I was writhing and screaming in pain, the 911 leader gave me an anti-pain shot as the rest of the crew was trying to get me on the folding wheeled stretcher to load me in the ambulance. The shot helped a little, but not much. The emergency room was ready for me. They had pulled my TMH record and determined that Dr. Hank Hutchinson had done my hip replacement surgery; someone there decided I should await his return on Monday (next day) for whatever surgery I needed. In my view, the delay was a mistake because he was not in his office until Thursday, when he saw my x-rays and ordered the surgery for Friday. Was the delay a mistake? All I know is that for the four-day delay, I was heavily medicated but had a high pain level that never went away. I also know they kept me totally immobile and that I developed bed sores on both heels. Despite constant attention by "wound doctors," both heels are still sensitive to pressure. Now comes the complex part of the healing process.

During all the blood analyses related to the hip surgery, the blood experts found bacteria which they could not identify and it was causing a blood infection. As always, we went into a heavy antibiotic medication program which, like all antibiotic regimes, tears up my insides. I became totally incontinent, lost complete control over my bodily functions, and had to be handled like a six-month-old baby. I wore adult diapers which had to be changed six times a day around the clock to avoid diaper rash and simply to keep me clean. You are entitled to ask, so what is the big deal about changing diapers? Babies usually love it! Well, here are the two reasons why diaper changing was an unpleasant event for me over a period of several months.

First, because I could not stand up or sit up, all changes had to be made with me in the prone position, on my back. To remove the used diaper and start the new one on, I had to roll over on my left side, with staff help, and after a couple of minutes, had to roll to the other side, with staff help. The left-side roll was slightly painful, but the right-side roll put heavy pressure on my surgery leg and really hurt. I had to do that six times a day and night and it was a continuing pain process over a period of months.

Second, there was the personal embarrassment and ego smashing situation wherein I am known all over the medical center as the Marine General of three wars and recipient of international awards, now lying without any clothes on, being cleaned up by young girls and boys who were students in an FSU nursing program. It simply was not like being treated by registered nurses and others who are professionals in the medical field, and I agonized over it every minute. I am an old-fashioned, Southern gentleman who totally respects women and young people, and I hated the physical exposure during my hospital time. Over that period of time, going through pain I didn't think my body could handle, I asked God several times out loud, in front of witnesses, to take me home to his Heavenly Kingdom because I didn't want to live with such pain. In hindsight, it is clear that He did not hear me, or He heard me and decided the time was not right, or, worst option of all, His Kingdom may not be my final destination.

Well, so much for the lows. Let's wind up by listing the highs which were wonderful despite all the physical lows which intruded in between. I will then do a wrap up to put a finish to the Snowden Story.

Despite all the physical miseries I suffered over the year, there were some lifetime highs that make it a time to remember. When Prime Minister Abe of Japan spoke to a Joint Session of Congress, it was a historical first. I was the guest of the Prime Minister, so I was invited to sit in the House Gallery where I was seated with Prime Minister Abe's wife, Ambassador Caroline Kennedy (US Ambassador to Japan), and the wife of Ambassador Sasae. On my other side was Diet Member Shindo (grandson of LtGen Kurabayashi, who commanded the Japanese troops on Iwo Jima), and my two sons, John Stephen and Brian.

About three minutes into his speech, the Prime Minister called out my name and asked me to stand and be recognized. As I stood and shook hands with Shindo-san, the Prime Minister thanked me for my work on the US-Japan relationship over the past twenty years (the Joint Reunion of Honor) and called it a "miracle of history." For me, an old country boy, it certainly was a high moment in my life.

Later, I was inducted into the Florida Veterans Hall of Fame, followed by a reception at the Governor's Mansion. Even later, I received the Stan Tate Leadership Award from the Economic Club of Florida. I was unable to be there, so the award was accepted for me by Brigadier General William Webb, USAF, Retired, a close and valued friend.

In March 2016 was the real highlight event, when the Commandant, General Bob Neller, and his wife flew to Tallahassee to present me with two medals: the Distinguished Public Service Award from the Secretary of Defense (the highest award SecDef can give) and the Distinguished Public Service Award from the Secretary of the Navy (the highest award he can give). In the McGuire Center at Westminster Oaks, before a standing-room-only audience of 450 neighbors and general public friends, General Neller presented me the two medals and gave me a framed copy of the Congressional Record in which I was cited as "a great American." The Commandant stole the show with his good humor, his very gracious remarks about me, and by singing the Marine Corps Hymn before he left the stage to mingle with the audience. I do not need any more of a highlight than that! And so, it is wrap-up time.

When Martha and I lived in Fullerton, California, on most Sundays we attended church services at the Crystal Cathedral where we heard some great sermons by some great pastors. No matter who preached, the opening line usually was, "This is a day the Lord has made, let us rejoice and be glad in it." That is the way I intend to live the rest of my life, celebrating each day as it comes and hope the good ones will outnumber the bad ones.

FINIS ~ FINITO ~ END OF SNOWDEN'S STORY

Appendices

Appendix I

Important Documents

Starting point for the Marines, April 17, 1942.

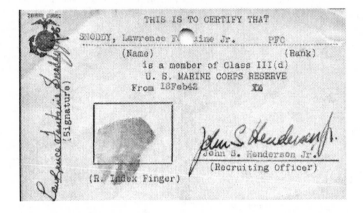

AF-360-hfb

HEADQUARTERS U. S. MARINE CORPS
WASHINGTON

17 April, 1942.

From: The Commandant, U. S. Marine Corps.
To: Private First Class **Lawrence F. Snoddy, Jr.**, USMCR,
      673 Evergreen Avenue, Charlottesville, Virginia.

Subject: Assignment to active duty to attend the
      Candidates' Class for Commission.

Enclosure: (A) Self-addressed envelope.

    1.   It is the intention of this Headquarters to
assign you to active duty to attend the Candidates' Class for
Commission which begins on **or about 11 May, 1942.**

    2.   You are hereby directed to report any change of
address which might have occurred after being enlisted for this
purpose, in order that the issuance of orders and your compliance
therewith may be expedited.

    3.   It is requested that the following information, in
duplicate, on the attached copies be furnished this Headquarters
IMMEDIATELY. A self-addressed envelope which requires no postage
is enclosed. Failure to reply immediately to this correspondence
may result in disciplinary action:

    (a) Address during the month of **April 1942:** _____

        673 Evergreen Avenue, Charlottesville, Virginia

    (b) Show name of railroad having passenger service from
        point that transportation is desired. If you do not
        live near a railroad, state name of bus company having
        connections with the nearest railroad: _____

        Southern Railroad

    4.   Transportation will be furnished from the address
shown in (a) above ONLY! Travel via privately owned conveyance
to the Marine Barracks, Quantico, Virginia, will NOT be allowed.

                               H. L. SCHIESSWOHL,
                               By direction.

The Boy Scouts of America awarded me the Distinguished Eagle Award in
1974.

FAR EAST COUNCIL   BOY SCOUTS OF AMERICA

CARRYING SCOUTING
TO THE FAR EAST

OFFICE TACHIKAWA AIR BASE BLDG 2740   PHONE TACHIKAWA A.B. 30883, 33885
TACHIKAWA JAPAN   MAIL APO SAN FRANCISCO 96323

20 February 1974

The Commandant
U.S. Marine Corps
Washington, D.C. 20380

Sir:

It gives me great pleasure to report that MG Lawrence F.
Snowden, Vice President of the Far East Council, was awarded
the Distinguished Eagle Award last Sunday evening at the Council
Annual Dinner.

This award, made by the National Court of Honor of the Boy
Scouts of America, recognizes men who, as boys, became Eagle
Scouts and who have distinguished themselves in their chosen
profession. It is one of the top awards made by our organization.

Since the award represents significant contributions to our
nation and its youth and to the Marine Corps, it might be appro-
priately recorded in MG Snowden's permanent file.

Sincerely,

HARRY A. HARCHAR
Scout Executive

HAH/ls
Encl: Citation

Following Pages: Release from active duty, May 1979.

MMSR-2/js
31 MAY 1979

From: Commandant of the Marine Corps
To: Lieutenant General Lawrence F. SNOWDEN 231 03 35 46/
9903 USMC
Via: Commanding Officer, Headquarters Battalion,
Headquarters, U. S. Marine Corps, Henderson Hall,
Arlington, Virginia 22214

Subj: Release from active duty and assignment to the Retired
List of officers of the Marine Corps

Ref: (a) Title 10, U. S. Code
(b) JTR, par M 4158
(c) IRAM, par 2003
(d) PRIM, par 5153

Encl: (1) Commission on the Retired List in the grade of
Lieutenant General
(2) Retired Pay Data Form
(3) Retirement Button
(4) Certificate of retirement
(5) CMC ltr MMSR-2/jec of 15 Jun 1978 w/encls

1. On 1 June 1979 you will be placed on the Marine Corps
Retired List in accordance with the provisions established
by reference (a). Accordingly, at 2400 31 May 1979 you
will be detached from your present duty station and released
from active duty. You will proceed to your home (MCC W95)
and complete all travel within the time specified in reference
(b). Active duty pay and allowances terminate 31 May 1979.

2. You have been appointed by the President and confirmed
by the Senate to the grade of lieutenant general on the Retired List pursuant to the provisions of reference (a). I
take pleasure in transmitting as enclosure (1) your commission
in the grade of lieutenant general. Your retired pay will be
based on that grade.

3. As of 31 May 1979 you will have completed 37 years, 3
months and 13 days accumulative service of which 37 years,
1 month and 4 days is active service.

4. The officer having custody of your records will:

a. Issue identification card pursuant to reference (c).

MMSR-2/js

Subj: Release from active duty and assignment to the
       Retired List of officers of the Marine Corps

    b. Enter on DD Form 214: "Tr to Ret'd List."

    c. Report retirement in accordance with reference (d).

5. TravChar appn 1791105.2754, MPMC-79, BCN 45690, AAA 27,
CC 74122 off tvl 74150 depns tvl 74152 trans HHG.

6. Enclosure (2) should be completed and forwarded to the
Marine Corps Finance Center. You cannot be paid until this
form is received by the Center. Enclosures (3) and (4) are
furnished for your retention.

7. Should you be found not physically qualified at time of
retirement these orders are cancelled and should be returned
to the Commandant of the Marine Corps (Code.MMSR) for dis-
position.

8. Please furnish the disbursing officer carrying your account
copies of these orders for settlement of your pay account.

9. Please keep the Marine Corps Finance Center, Retired Pay
Division, Kansas City, Missouri 64197 informed of your current address.

10. The statement of employment (DD Form 1357) enclosure
(5) should be completed within thirty days after date of
retirement and forwarded to the Marine Corps Finance Center.

                        LOUIS H. WILSON

Copy to:
Officer Addressed (40)
MARCORFINCTR (Code CPR)
CMC Code MPI
CMC Code MMPR-3
CMC Code HQSH
CMC Code LA
CMC Code FD
CMC Code MMPR
CMC Code MMOA
CMC Code MMAD-3

ORIGINAL ORDERS

UNITED STATES MARINE CORPS
Company "B"
Headquarters Battalion
Headquarters, Marine Corps
Henderson Hall
Arlington, Virginia 22214

MWS:dlt
1800.1
31 May 1979

FIRST ENDORSEMENT on CMC LtrO MMSR-2/js of 31 May 1979

From: Commanding Officer
To: Lieutenant General Lawrence F. SNOWDEN 231033546

Subj: Release from Active Duty and Transfer to the Retired List

1. Delivered.

2. Your unused leave to include date of release from active duty will be as follows:

60.0 Days Saved Leave Balance
00.0 Days Regular Leave Balance

Settlement for your unused leave will be included in your final active duty pay check.

3. The last place to which you were furnished or reimbursed for dependent transportation was: Washington D. C. 20390.

4. You have been issued an identification card in accordance with reference (c).

5. You have given as your forwarding address:

5007 Woodland Way
Annandale, VA. 22003

C. E. RICHARDS JR.

Copy to:
CMC (MMSR-2, MPI, MMPR-3, HQSH, LA, MMPR, MMOA, MMAD-3, INTS)
MCFC, Code CPR, KSC (2)

```
                                                             MWS:dlt
                                                             1800.1

Subj:   Release from Active Duty and Transfer to the Retired List

 Copy to:  (continued)
MCDO, WASHDC (2)
Mail Room, Navy Annex
PhysExamRm, Navy Annex
OQR
File
-----------------------------------------------------------------
Received these orders at "B" Company, HqBn, HQMC, HH, ARLVA 22214 at
1400  on  31 May 1979.


                            Lawrence F. Snowden
                          LAWRENCE F. SNOWDEN
```

Note from President Carter, 1978.

THE WHITE HOUSE

WASHINGTON

August 5, 1978

To General Lawrence Snowden

Rosalynn and I appreciated the warm hospitality
extended to us last night, and particularly enjoyed
seeing the Marine Corps Sunset Parade.

We enjoyed being with you and Martha. Thank you
for your efforts in our behalf.

Sincerely,

Jimmy

A note of thanks from Florida Governor Lawton Chiles, 1995.

STATE OF FLORIDA

Office of the Governor

THE CAPITOL
TALLAHASSEE, FLORIDA 32399-0001

LAWTON CHILES
GOVERNOR

December 29, 1995

General Lawrence Snowden
4040 Esplanade Way
Building *B* / Suite 260
Tallahassee, Florida 32399-7000

Dear General Snowden:

Just a note to say how much I enjoyed participating in your Leadership Seminar at Wakulla Springs.

General, the picture of the soaring eagle you presented me with certainly has an important message. I appreciate getting it, and I have a special place in mind to hang it.

Again, it was good to be with you and your group. Keep up the good work you are doing, and please feel free to give me a call if I can ever be of assistance.

With kind personal regards, I am

Sincerely,

LAWTON CHILES

LC/adf

THE JAPAN LETTER

Number 266

15 April 1984

Dear Sir:

AMERICAN AMBASSADOR TO JAPAN, MIKE MANSFIELD, is well past the normal retirement age.

And he would have been retired long ago were it not for the respect and popularity he commands with the Japanese, the American business community in Tokyo, adminstration officials in Washington and his former congressional colleagues.

Still, though, nobody can last forever and even the most avid Mansfield supporters in Washington are beginning to think seriously about his replacement.

A few names have been considered so far. And others will be considered before a recommendation is placed before the president for nomination as Mansfield's successor.

What they are looking for is someone who can be tough without being abrasive, who has some experience in dealing with the Japanese but who also has experience and some clout in Washington.

So, they really are not looking for a career ambassador---although there are some who argue that the post should go to a career man----but a high powered business executive or politican.

Or, maybe an ex-military man?

Don't scoff at that idea.

The leading candidate at the moment is a former military man.

And in the relatively short time that he has been out of the military he has proven himself to be as adept in the business world as he was in the military.

When it comes to diplomacy he also has shown that a lot of career men might be able to learn something from him.

So, who are we talking about?

Retired U.S. Marine General LAWRENCE F. SNOWDEN, that's who.

He currently is based in Tokyo as Far East Area Vice President for Hughes Aircraft International Service Company.

He has served as President of the American Chamber of Commerce in Japan as well as a Special Advisor to the Advisory Council on U.S.-Japan Relations.

As a Marine, he served for three years in the early 1970's as Chief of Staff of U.S. Forces in Japan and concurrently as the U.S. Chairman of the U.S.-Japan Joint Committee.

There's much more background that we could cite. But the point is made. Snowden is a man who knows what it is all about in Japan.

And when his name has been mentioned to top level Japanese business, government and political leaders as a possible candidate to succeed Mansfield, the reaction has been extremely favorable.

So our informants say.

In fact, they say it would not be wrong to characterize the reaction of most of them as "enthusiastic".

Congressional Record - Recognizing Lt. General Lawrence F. Snowden, 02 February 2016. *

*The text can be found at https://www.congress.gov/crec/2016/
02/02/CREC-2016-02-02-pt1-PgE96-3.pdf. Photo ©M.R. Street.

Appendix II

Speech delivered 28 August 1962

Delivered to 28   28 Aug
Assembled Bn - in Aug 62   62

I have had you assembled here this morning for several purposes. 1st I want to tell you something about me. 2d I want to explain some of my basic philosophy to you about how this battalion will operate in the future and 3d I want to tell you about the general training schedule which faces us over the next several months.

① <u>About me</u>:

Why do I want to tell you about me? I consider this a fair exchange of information because I have all of your Service records available for study but mine is not available to you. Basically too I agree with the Will Rogers philosophy that to know a man is to like him and I want our relationship to be favorable from the outset.

I was a senior at the University of Va when Pearl

Harbor occurred. I had
already been in touch
with Marine Officer Procurement
Teams and I was instructed
to sit tight until they called
me. I was called in May
1942 and sent to Quantico
in the Officer Candidate
Program. After Officers School
I went to Camp Lejeune
to join the 3rd Marine Division.
My regiment, dropped out
of The 3rd Division to
act as nucleus of the 4th
Division. We split into two
regiments and came out
here to Camp Pendleton to
form as the 4th Marine Division.
      With the 4th Division
I was a Platoon Leader,
was a Co Exec when we
landed in the Roi-Namur
Islands in early 1944. I was
a Company commander
at Saipan, Tinian and at
Iwo Jima. When the war
ended I was on Guam preparing
for invasion of the Japanese
main land and had the uneasy
feeling that my number might
be coming up during that next round.

After getting back home I
went to Headquarters Marine
Corps for three years. From
there I was drew a one
year assignment to North-
western University to obtain
a masters degree in Personnel
Administration and Training.
From there to Quantico
to assist in establishing the
Marine Corps Development
Center and the Joint Landing
Force Board. From Quantico
I went to Korea for my first
tour with the 1st Marine
Division. There I served
as Regimental S-4 for the
7th Marines, later as Executive
Officer of the 1st Bn, 7th
Marines and later as Assistant
G-4 on the Division Staff.

From Korea to New
York City as OIC of the
MC Recruiting Station for
two years. I wound up
that tour as a physical
mess. During a snow storm
a fellow hit my car head
on and I lost my left
knee cap. That leg is so good

now that I'm thinking of taking the right knee cap out too! In any event this will explain the basketball knee guard you'll see me wear from time to time.

From New York City, to Paris, France where I served in the Headquarters of the United States European Command, headed up by General Norstad. After two years in Paris I returned to Senior School in Quantico for a year and then back to Headquarters Marine Corps where I've been for the past three years prior to my reporting here.

I am now in my 21st year of Service. I have been in my present rank since 1 January 1975 and ready or not I come before a selection board next August for possible selection for Colonel. My performance with this Battalion

will have a direct bearing
on my chances for selection
come next August. If I bust
my breeches here I've had
the course.

I have been married
for almost 20 years and
have one son 18 and
another one 12 — or one
son per war.

Well so much for
my military background.
Let me conclude this
first phase by saying that
I am very happy to be
here. It is a job I've waited
for for about 8 years and
I propose to work it for
the good of the Marine Corps,
for your good and my
own good — and in that
precise order.

"Now 2d — I want to spend a few ~~couple of~~ minutes to aquaint you with certain fundamental philosophy about how this battalion will operate.

First of all, understand that the company commanders and the individual companies are important cogs in our battalion machinery. It is at the company level that ~~the battalion gets~~ the battalion gets its real punch and it is my job, assisted by the battalion staff, to

ensure that the Companies work
together and fight together, as a battalion
supported by other units such
as artillery, engineers, aviation
and other support units that
might be made available
to us by higher authority.

This last Friday saw
the completion of the first
lock-on phase of training
for this battalion. Your
emphasis has been on
small unit training. During
the next phase we get into
amphibious training, helicopter

training and battalion
size problems, both as an
independent battalion and
as a part of a larger force.
You will find that our
success as a battalion will
depend a great deal on
how well you execute the
small unit tactics which you
have been learning in the
first phase. The basic strength of a Marine
Corps effectiveness has been
in individual proficiency
and team work between units.
I am a great believer
in the theory that if we
will solve all of our little
problems with prompt and

decisive action that we
won't have many big problems
to solve. All of you know
full well that our military
system is built on a
system of discipline and
prompt response to orders.
This means that when
you receive an order you
don't argue, you execute. If
there is any question about
the propriety of the order that
point can be settled later.

I hope I will not
be required to spend a great

amount of time on legal
matters and investigations.
I expect some, cases but I hope that
there will be
very few. In regard to
legal matters I mention
the following basic points
In disciplinary matters
a - this is not a three
strike league. One strike
might put you out of
the ball game. This is particularly
applicable to any marine who
fails to carry out his
responsibility for his men and
their welfare.
2 - with regard to NCOs
I charge every one of you
to recognize the authority that

is vested in non-commissioned
officers. Remember that
they are officers. Though
they are not commissioned
by the Congress, they have
official authority over
personnel of lesser ranks
and are to be obeyed
accordingly. It will be
our policy and practice
to insure that non-commissioned
officers are given responsibility
commensurate with their
rank and that their
authority is respected.

~~If~~ a member of
this command becomes
involved with civil or other
military authorities we will
do what we can to assist
~~him~~ and to insure that
he is ~~not~~ afforded
~~the~~ the rights to which

he is
~~gra Ceo~~ entitled. In
particular to you younger
Marine's I want to stress
the importance of keeping
your service record free
of office hours and all other
unfavorable matter.
~~Special of particular~~. Whether
you make a career of the
Marine Corps or put in just
one enlistment, a clean
record will serve to your
personal advantage. To
the old hands who have
had their overseas tour
I remind you that your

record ~~could~~ <u>can</u> have a direct
influence on your next
duty assignment. To the
younger hands who will
rotate ~~~~ overseas, ~~~~ ^{with the Battalion} ~~~~
I urge you to keep your
record clean so you don't
start that part of your tour
with a strike or ~~two~~ against
you. I assure you that I
want to get to know ~~all~~
of you but I am not
eager to get aquainted with
~~any of~~
you via the office hours
routine

d   Officers and men alike
must realize that higher
authority at reg't and Div
and back to HQMC requires
us to report statistical data
of all kinds. For example
we must report the number
of men who are enrolled
in after hours education courses,
the number of traffic violations,
the number of men at
sick call and lots of these
kinds of reports. Lets not lose
sight of the fact that these
statistics are not goals in

themselves. We will view them
for what they are — indicators
of performance of the officers
and men of the battalion.
I want to see a lot of
you enrolled in off-duty
education classes and a
lot of you out for the
various athletic teams — not
because the statistics are
important but because these
programs offer you opportunity
for self-improvement and I
want to see you take
advantage of these opportunities.

c. A point which is already of concern to me is the consumption of alcoholic beverages. It has been only recently that beer has been made available in the clubs for the lower ranks. Part of the justification for permitting beer in the clubs was that any man who was mature enough to fight for his country was mature enough to be treated as an adult in other ways. I agree with the basic theory but I am concerned about how some Marines want the privileges but don't want the responsibility associated with maturity. The problem becomes acute when the alcohol is mixed with an automobile. As the slogans say, alcohol and autos don't mix. It is my hope that officers and men alike will enjoy the clubs

to the fullest. At the same
time, I hope you will
monitor your own consumption
of alcohol so that you
don't get yourself and others
in trouble. ~~Once again, I
hope you will check each
other, recognizing that~~ We
will continue to emphasize vehicle
safety and good driving
habits and hope you will
~~_____~~ benefit accordingly.

e. A final point related
to my basic philosophy
about operating this battalion.
I intend to use all
authority available to me
to effect promotions and
to insure that the more
senior men are helped
toward promotion by rendering
appropriate fitness reports on
them. These things must be
deserved however. Further,
and directly related, will be
the policy to examine closely
those rated men who do

not perform their duties
satisfactorily. In such cases
efforts will be made to
reduce their rates in order
that the rates may be given
to those with greater potential. In this
connection I agree with
the philosophy expressed by
General Shoup who said
that promotions are partly
as a reward but even more
promotions
should recognize future
potential and capability.

Now 3rd — lets discuss
briefly our training schedule
for the next several
months. We are due for
surf indoctrination this
week. It has been necessary
to postpone our wet net
training for a while however.
We will have a chance to
fire these M14s and
establish a new high in
percentage of qualification.
In September we participate
in a /SELREX which will
take us aboard an aircraft carrier

for a helicopter landing.
We have a chance to
participation in a Division
CPX. Concurrently, in
September we will be
preparing for the Division
Commanders inspection
which is scheduled for
19 October. That will be
preceded by our own
inspection and an inspection
by the Regimental Commander
both intended to help us get
ready for the Commanding
Generals inspection. On

1 November we become
the ready BLT and
between then a 31 December
we'll be the first to move
if Marines are required from
this Division! Also coming
up are Company Tactical
Tests, a Battalion Tactical
Test, ~~and~~ Cold Weather
Training at Pickle Meadows
and a Division/Wing
exercise after the first of
the new calendar year.
In the Spring we get a
crack at training in the desert.

All of these things should
have us in tip top shape
as a battalion. In late
spring of course we
lose our older hands
to schools, posts and
stations and other places.
You younger hands then
become the old hands, we
take on a new group of
Marines and prepare for
rotation overseas next fall.

~~I have indicated my~~
~~willingness to take this~~
~~battalion overseas but so~~

mixed in with the
heavy training schedule
which will be hard work
there is a fair amount of
relaxation and hard play.
We have a leaders night
coming up for fire team
leaders and above, the
Marine Corps birthday parties
are being planned now, the
Fall athletic program is
about to get underway and
other recreational and
social events are being considered.
Liberty will be available to you to the
extent that our commitments will allow.

~~the early to discuss that~~

~~point~~

Men, our work is
cut out for us. The
demands are going to be
heavy but I am confident
that individually, as company my section
we will be up to the
task. Further I'm confident we can
do it and have a good time ~~tonight~~.
In conclusion I want
to express my official
and my personal appreciation
to you for a fine parade
this past Friday As you
marched past the receiving
stand I became very much

aware of the responsibility
I have to you as your
battalion commander. I shall attempt
to meet those responsibilities
full measure.

With your support,
and God willing, we
will do what I've already
promised the Regimental
Commander. I promised him
we would run the Thundering
Third to the top of the Division
flag pole and that's what
we're going to do!

Co Cmdrs, take charge of your Companies.

→ We will assemble as a battalion from time to time in order that I can speak to you personally about our programs. I hope to keep you informed as to what is coming up and why we do the things that we do. I believe that an informed Marine is a better Marine — I will attempt to keep you informed.

Appendix III

Iwo Jima Battle Revisited, 2005

Basic Text of Remarks by
Lawrence F. Snowden
Lieutenant General, U.S. Marine Corps, Retired

60th Anniversary Dinner
Celebrating the Victory at Iwo Jima

Marine Memorial Club
San Francisco, California

Wednesday, 23 February 2005

Thank you, General Myatt, and thank all of you for that very warm reception. I have visited this club several times over the years, but my longest stay here was in 1953 as I was headed to Korea. I was ordered to report to the Department of the Pacific at 100 Harrison Street for further transportation to Korea. Three other majors whom I knew were already here, so we were a tight-knit group for those five days. Our problem was that each of us had very little money, we had left any money we had with our wives, and we had not counted on delaying five days in the great city of San Francisco. Two things saved us after the first night here. The "Paymaster" at 100 Harrison Street was LtCol Nick Lengel, whom I had known from a previous tour at Headquarters, Marine Corps. Each morning, the four of us would get over to 100 Harrison Street and Nick would advance one day's pay to each of us. We got a further break when we were joined by Major Bernie Bernardini, a reservist and a member of a great Greek family which was big in commercial fishing in San Diego. The difference was that Bernie had company credit cards and none of the rest of us had credit cards in those days. With Bernie's generosity, we enjoyed our time in the bar on the upper floor of this fine club, we enjoyed the Yankee Doodle Bar, just a short distance away, and then we enjoyed a lot of great food at several first-class restaurants. It was a great delay en route.

I greatly appreciate the opportunity to join with you tonight in celebrating the victory on Iwo Jima sixty years ago. Every day since I left that island on 26 March 1945 has been a bonus in my life, and if God calls me home to the Big Marine Corps Base in the Sky before this night is over, I will have no complaints when I knock at the Golden Gate, assuming that is where I am going.

This is a very special Iwo Jima celebration because of the presence of Joe Rosenthal, who took the picture which is the most widely recognized picture in the world today. The victory at Iwo Jima would have been historic by any standard, but I think we have to recognize that it was Joe Rosenthal's magnificent picture which gave the event more attention than it could have gotten any other way. A true case in which one picture was worth at least ten thousand words and made it such a memorable event.

At the Iwo Jima Memorial in Arlington, the base of the monument has Marine Corps battles inscribed, but there are only two individual names on the base of the monument. Those names are Felix de Weldon, sculptor, and Joe Rosenthal, photographer. All Marines will be forever grateful to you, Joe Rosenthal, for capturing that special moment in our history and for bringing the Iwo Jima battle to the forefront of epic battles of World War II.

Sixty years after the bloodiest battle of World War II, what is there to say about Iwo Jima? Certainly, I cannot add anything that military historians and Marine authors have not already said about the strategic value of that little island and the tactics which were employed by the ground forces as we moved from the area of Mount Suribachi to the northern tip of the island. About the most I can do is tell you about a couple of my memories from that hell on earth experience. But, most importantly, I can verify to you as an up-close witness that the young Marines who fought on Iwo Jima truly earned the right to be called "The Greatest Generation."

For my own part, I was just there, a 23-year-old captain, trying to do what the Marine Corps had trained me to do. In command of a rifle company of 200 young Marines, my job was to receive orders from my battalion commander, give orders to my platoon leaders who were entrusted to move the troops to objectives or areas deemed necessary to defeat the defenders and bring the island under control. It was my job to ensure that they received artillery fire support, close air support, tank support, or whatever firepower was needed to support their advance.

For the first twenty-four hours or so, the primary objectives were to stay alive and try to get our units together so we could fight as we had been trained to fight, as fire teams, as squads, platoons, and companies. Under the dreadful and constant fire of the defenders, moving about and establishing contact was close to impossible, but somehow we managed to get reasonably well organized on that second day. On D-Day, some 30,000 Marines were put ashore between 9:15 a.m. and about 5:00 p.m. The cost was high – more than 2000 casualties.

At the company level, our intelligence about the island was somewhat less than perfect, but that was and is now, usually the case. First, the estimated size of the defending force was about half of what we encountered. A quote from my Battalion Operation Plan read, "Workman Island is reported to be defended by a force of 12,000 to 14,000, including infantry, artillery, tanks, engineers, and airbase personnel." The defending force was really 23,000. That force suffered very little attrition because of their use of caves, reinforced bunkers, and deep underground tunnels and assembly rooms.

Second, there simply was no appreciation about how difficult it would be to move over the beaches in the soft volcanic ash and sand, how difficult it would be for men and vehicles to climb the steep sand ridges, referred to as terraces, or how difficult it would be for the LVTs to move off the beach. The landing plan was based on the premise that those of us in the LVTs would drive right on across the beach and reach that first airfield in pretty quick time. In some cases, the LVTs were unable to get past the first sand terrace. It was extremely difficult for the troops to dig foxholes to get themselves beneath the ground level seeking to get some modest protection against the tremendous firepower being thrown at us by the Japanese defenders.

The intelligence annex to the operation plan stated clearly that the loose sand and volcanic ash soil was 10 feet deep in parts of the island, but somehow, none of us realized how troublesome that soil could be. We were not helped by a line in the annex which I quote, "Personnel and vehicles should have no difficulties from natural obstacles in crossing the area except for the anti-tank obstacles." The quote, "natural obstacles," unquote, of deep volcanic ash and sand, along with the three steep sand terraces, made the beaches extremely difficult for us.

My LVT went inland for only fifty yards or so, spun to the left on its tracks, and came to a halt. I yelled, "Bail out," and we all jumped over the side. In those days, there was no top cover on the LVTs. I jumped into the nearest bomb crater and came face to face with Sergeant Leonard Ash. One of his legs was badly shattered. Leonard said, "Captain, please help me." I said, "Len, I will give you a shot of morphine and then I have to get moving." He said, "I have already used my morphine," so I said, "Len, I'll try to get a corpsman." I turned toward the rear and shouted, "Corpsman, Corpsman!" An unknown voice replied, "On the way." With that, I did what the Marine Corps had drilled into me, but it was one of the hardest things I ever had to do, to leave Len Ash while he was suffering so. I said, "Len, a corpsman is on the way. I have to get moving. Good luck." When I saw Sergeant Le ash twenty-five years later and saw that he still had that leg, I was astounded but delighted. He had six operations on that leg and two knee replacements over those twenty-five years, but walked good enough to play a slow game of golf. Len is now deceased, but next month on the trip to Iwo Jima, Gregg Ash, his son, will be in the group and I will walk with him to the area where his father was wounded. The Len Ash story does not stop there. Len died of a heart attack as he was starting to speak against a rally of war protestors in Orange Park, Florida. The story of his death and the remarks he intended to make are in the Congressional Record.

Lieutenant General Kuribayashi and his troops did a good job on the beaches. They let the first two waves get ashore with relatively light fire, but as my third wave, the second wave of troops, hit the beach, they opened up with guns of every caliber when they had us in their designated target areas. Every square meter of the beaches had been zeroed in and with the great observation advantage from Mount Suribachi and other high spots, with troops moving slowly in the powdery sand, it was a real turkey shoot for them.

Two final comments about the sands of Iwo Jima. An unidentified lieutenant wrote in our 4th Marine Division book these words, "It was impossible to dig a hole. The gravel was too slippery, too shifting, and powder light, too formless; it was dry as quicksand and sucked at everything touching it, filling every hole as soon as it was formed."

One other comment about the volcanic sand. Back in the Old Corps, each rifle company headquarters included two buglers, proper title, field musics. When not bugling, they were runners for the company commander. On D+1, my two field musics and I were in a bomb crater on the edge of the first airfield in mid-afternoon. One of our naval gunfire ships fired a short 5-inch round which landed about thirty yards to the right of my position and adjacent to a bomb crater in which there were two corpsmen. The two of them were completely buried by the volcanic ash and sand. Several of us ran over to their crater and started digging them out. We got one out, but the other one smothered to death in that powdery sand before we could get him out. Neither of them was wounded by the naval shell, but the black sands of Iwo Jima claimed another victim.

The third intelligence flaw related to the lack of effectiveness of our aerial bombardment and the heavy rounds of our naval gunfire. Despite thousands of aerial bombs delivered by the Army Air Corps and naval aircraft, and more than 20,000 rounds of heavy naval shells from our battleships and heavy cruisers, the 23,000 defenders emerged from their caves and tunnels and poured thousands of rounds of every caliber on those of us trying to move inland. General "Howling Mad" Smith had wanted the Navy to provide another five days of shelling of the island, but the Navy commanders were under tremendous pressure from elements of the Japanese fleet in the area and said they couldn't spare the ships to do that. With their deep tunnels, huge assembly rooms deep down in the innards of that island, the defenders seemed oblivious to American bombing and shelling.

By the end of the second day, it was pretty clear that Iwo Jima could only be taken yard by yard, and the estimate of ten days for the operation was overly optimistic. Our most effective weapon was the flamethrower, followed by satchel charges and grenades to burn, blast, and bomb the defenders out of their pillboxes and caves. All of these weapons had to be delivered close up by the Marine grunts, and that made all the ground combat very close combat. When the defenders would rush out of a cave or a camouflaged defense position, they would rush right into the foxholes and bomb craters and slash away at whoever was in there. For hundreds of young Marines, the combat knife became the instrument of survival.

By the night of 23 February, the 28th Marines had reached the base of Suribachi, and on the morning of the 24th, Iwo Jima time, a combat patrol began working their way up the back side of the mountain. When they reached the top, they found a piece of water pipe and the first flag was raised. You know the rest of the story about the second flag raising and the tremendous morale boost it was for the Marines on the island and the Navy aboard the many ships to see Old Glory flying from that mountaintop. I have read accounts which said that every Marine on the island stood up and cheered when that flag became visible from that mountaintop. I can tell you, and Dale Cook, present here tonight, a member of my company at that time, will verify for you, if you were in

Fox Company, you didn't stand up because we were in close contact with some heavy defenses, and standing up was the last thing you wanted to do. Standing up would have insured that it was your last action on Earth.

There were many heroes on Iwo Jima, some were recognized by medals, but there were many who performed heroic acts above and beyond the call of duty but were not recipients of medals because there are many faults in the system of recommending and approving medal awards. I want to share with you the story of one young Marine, a true hero, who seems to me to epitomize the character of so many of the young Marines who fought on Iwo Jima.

My story is about a young Marine named Ernest Thomas, known to everyone as Boots. Boots was born in Tallahassee, Florida, but grew up in the much smaller town of Monticello, Florida, just 23 miles east of Tallahassee. In high school, Boots was the Big Man on Campus in a very small school. He had an IQ at the top of the scale and was president of his class. He was captain of the football team, captain of the basketball team, played on the baseball team and was in every school play. He went on to Liberty College to study engineering and was there at the time of Pearl Harbor.

Though encouraged to stay in school, Boots, like so many other young men at that time, felt a strong obligation to get into the military and help win the war. Boots decided he wanted to be a Marine, so he went to the nearest Armed Forces Examining Station but was rejected because he was colorblind. He went to another examining station and was rejected again. But Boots figured out the system. On his third try, he stood up close to the fellow ahead of him as he took the color test. Boots memorized the sequence of the color cards and passed the test. He went to Parris Island and, after his first five weeks there, his company commander recommended him for officer training at Quantico. He had to take another physical, and Headquarters Marine Corps said no, he was colorblind. Boots finished his recruit training and joined the 5th Marine Division as it was in its formative stage.

The next time we hear about Boots, he is a platoon sergeant in the 28th Marines. As the 28th Marines fought their way to the base of Mount Suribachi, Boots repeatedly exposed himself to enemy fire as he called for tank support against a heavily fortified position. He was later recommended for the Navy Cross for his action. Boots was the platoon sergeant who, in the absence of his wounded platoon leader, led the combat patrol up the back side of Mount Suribachi, and it was Boots who found the piece of Japanese water pipe that became the flagpole. In the picture taken of the first flag raising, Boots is the Marine in the foreground, standing with his rifle at the ready to protect the flag raisers.

General Smith ordered Boots out to the flagship to do an interview that would be radio relayed to the States. The general wanted some good news to be given to the American public after the very bad news of the heavy casualties on the first two days. After the interview, Boots was headed back ashore in a small boat, and a press representative said to Boots, "How is it in there, really?" Boots said, "It is hell in there. My 21st birthday is coming up next week, and I don't expect to make it." Well, Boots was right; he didn't make it.

Three days later, he is leading his platoon again. He is down on one knee, rifle in his hand and radio in the other hand as he is calling for tank support against a heavily fortified bunker.

Those who witnessed it said that a sniper round hit Boots' rifle and knocked it out of his hand, but Boots did not stop talking on the radio. Less than two minutes later, a second sniper bullet caught him in the face, and Boots was gone.

Boots still has family in the Monticello area, and his sister is in an assisted living facility in Tallahassee. I saw her just two weeks ago, and she gave me a picture of Boots Thomas wearing his khaki uniform, on leave in Tallahassee, just before going overseas with the Fifth Division.

Boots Thomas, in my view, personifies the young Marines who were motivated by patriotism, chose the Marine Corps because it offered the most challenge, and he used his talents to the maximum when fighting for his country. A basic point about the Boots Thomas story is that we can measure the cost of war in terms of bombs, bullets, tanks, ships, and other material things, but we cannot measure the cost of the lost potential of young men and women like Boots Thomas and what they could have done for their hometowns, their states, and their nation.

There were other Boots Thomases on Iwo Jima, and there are others in our Armed Forces today. It is the best argument there is for finding a way to avoid war.

Next month, some of us will observe the 60th anniversary of our victory on Iwo Jima in a Reunion of Honor with the Japanese. While we are on that island on 12 March, we will not be celebrating our victory but will join with just a few, less than six, Japanese survivors and family members of those who lost their lives there as we honor those on both sides who gave their lives in service to their country. I will speak on behalf of the United States survivors. I will say that none of us who were there sixty years ago wanted to be there, but were there because our national leaders and our military leaders put us there, and each of us had to do what was necessary at the time. I plan to say that war breeds hatred, and hatred was in our hearts sixty years ago. I will also say that peace should breed friendships, and that is exactly what has happened in the sixty intervening years between the United States and Japan. Since the end of the war, the Japan-United States relationship has been the most important bilateral relationship in the world, and Japan has been our strong ally militarily, politically, and economically. The so-called trade friction wars of the 1980s were merely a blip on the radar.

After my remarks, a prominent political figure from Tokyo will make some remarks, and the Japanese will then perform the water pouring ceremony. Several family members of those who lost their lives there will circle the Peace Monument and pour consecrated water around the base of the monument to ease the thirst of all those who died of thirst – and there were many Japanese defenders who did. Each side will then lay a wreath on the monument, the national anthems of both nations will be played, and Taps will be sounded.

After the ceremony, there will be a brief period in which Marines give back to the Japanese side flags, photos, and other items they picked up on the battlefield. The Japanese are most appreciative of those returns. The Japanese side will then move up to the top of Mount Suribachi, where they have a small monument, and conduct a brief memorial service of their own. After that, they head back for the airfield and back to Tokyo via Air Self Defense Force aircraft.

Then the American side goes up to the top of Mount Suribachi to our monument. Everyone gets a reminder of how the defenders had such great observation over all of us coming across the beaches and see why they had a real turkey shoot for the first couple of days. There are always some active-duty Marines who want to re-enlist on the top of Suribachi, and others who want their pictures taken with some of the Old Corps Marines. After that, the Marine trucks start a round robin tour of seven or eight battle sites on the island. The Okinawa Marines build wooden steps on the back of the five-ton trucks so the old Marines can get aboard, and there are six or seven young Marines standing by at every truck stop to help the old Marines get on and off the trucks.

In earlier reunions, both sides gathered at the Peace Monument to share a few beers and some snacks, but some overly sensitive bureaucrat in Tokyo stopped that event. He was afraid that old adversaries, fueled by beer under a hot sun, might lose their composure and cause some unfavorable incident. He could not have been more wrong – We have never had the slightest suggestion of an unfavorable incident.

Around 5 o'clock, we have to start rounding up the old Marines who are bounding around in the brush, trying to find a spot they remember in their minds. It is imperative that we are off the island before dark, headed back to Guam.

For those survivors who go back to the island for the first time, it is an emotional experience. On every trip, I have several old Marines come to me with tears in their eyes and say, "General, I wasn't sure I wanted to make this trip, but I am so glad that I did." I have had them put their head on my shoulder and just sob. And so it will be next month.

My own guess is that this next Reunion of Honor will be the last one. It cannot turn into a purely commercial tour because of the special permission required to use the military facilities there. The Marine Corps these days is spread so very thin with its Middle East and other worldwide deployments, it is increasingly difficult for the Marine Corps and the reduced naval forces in the Marianas to provide all the support needed for the one-day event. Finally, the number of survivors who are still alive are in declining physical condition, and many find the cost of the tour a little hard to handle.

I was twice wounded on Iwo Jima, and why God allowed me to get out of there alive while so many of my Marine and Navy brothers died is more than I can understand. Whatever God's plan is for me, he better get me on to it real soon, because I may be starting to run out of time.

Over past years when I have spoken to veterans groups or civic groups about World War II or about Iwo Jima, I am always asked, "General, do you think our present generation of young people would perform like the 1940s Greatest Generation did? My answer consistently was the same; there is no doubt in my mind that they will. In 1941, we were motivated by Pearl Harbor. Today's youngsters only need to be motivated. Well, I have been proved right. Motivated by the 9/11 international terrorist attack and further motivated by the war in Iraq, our young men and women in the regular Armed Forces, in the Reserves, or in the National Guard, and whether or not they think the war in Iraq is justified, are serving courageously and with great patriotism, many of them losing arms or legs and will carry the scars of war for the rest of their lives. Over 1,600 have given their lives. When I ask God to bless America with young generations who are willing to serve their nation, I know he is already doing just that. We should all pray that he will continue to bless America in that way.

Thank you for the opportunity to share this great evening with you. Semper Fidelis and long live the Corps.

Appendix IV

Decorations and Medals*

Secretary of Defense Distinguished Public Service Award

Secretary of the Navy Distinguished Public Service Award

Distinguished Service Medal w/Gold Star

Legion of Merit w/4 Gold Stars and Combat V

Purple Heart Medal w/Gold Star

Joint Service Commendation Medal

Navy Commendation Medal w/1 bronze star

Army Commendation Medal

Asiatic Service Medal

Presidential Unit Citation w/3 bronze stars

Navy Unit Commendation w/1 bronze star

American Campaign Medal

Asiatic Pacific Campaign Medal w/4 bronze stars

Combat Action Ribbon

World War II Victory

National Defense Medal w/1 bronze star

Korean Service Medal w/2 bronze stars

Armed Forces Expeditionary Medal

Vietnam Service Medal w/2 bronze stars

Vietnam Cross of Gallantry w/Palm and 2 gold stars

Japanese 2nd Order of Sacred Treasure

Korean Presidential Unit Citation

Republic of Vietnam Armed Forces Meritorious Unit Citation Cross of Gallantry Color with Palm and frame

United Nations Service Medal

Republic of Vietnam Campaign Medal

Korean War Service Medal

---

* Listed in order of seniority/precedence for mounting medals, ribbons, other award devices

About My Collaborator, M.R. Street

Snowden's Story would not be in its present format without the expertise, skills, and dedication of my collaborator, M.R. Street. When I had finished writing all I wanted to write, all I had was a pile of typewritten pages and without any idea how to turn that pile into a book; nor did I have any ideas about adding pictures to the text.

My good friend, Commander Dennis Baker, USN, Retired, a published author, came to my rescue. He knew about M.R. as a writer and agent, so he told her about me and told me about her and with a phone call we arranged our first meeting. At the outset I knew I would be working with a winner. M.R. has a sincere smile and an easy-going personality, and she had all the experience and know-how that I lacked in order to produce a book. Thanks to her patience and her experience, we worked very well together.

So, M.R., the words may be mine but the book is yours because without you, the book would not exist. The book is your product and I will be forever indebted to you. I believe you have a bright future as a writer and agent and you will have my support and best wishes for success all along the way.

To M.R., thanks a ton. I treasure your friendship.

Larry Snowden